KEEP CALM AND TREAT ADDICTION

Your 12-Step Guide to Client Recovery

TANIA KELLY

First published by Ultimate World Publishing 2020
Copyright © 2020 Tania Kelly

ISBN

Paperback - 978-1-922372-50-5
Ebook - 978-1-922372-51-2

Tania Kelly has asserted her right under the Copyright, Designs and Patents Act 1988 to be identified as the author of this work. The information in this book is based on the author's experiences and opinions. The publisher specifically disclaims responsibility for any adverse consequences, which may result from use of the information contained herein. Permission to use information has been sought by the author. Any breaches will be rectified in further editions of the book.

All rights reserved. No part of this publication may be reproduced, stored in or introduced into a retrieval system, or transmitted in any form, or by any means (electronic, mechanical, photocopying, recording or otherwise) without the prior written permission of the author. Any person who does any unauthorised act in relation to this publication may be liable to criminal prosecution and civil claims for damages. Enquiries should be made through the publisher.

Cover design: Ultimate World Publishing
Layout and typesetting: Ultimate World Publishing
Editor: Marinda Wilkinson
llustrations: Ruxandra Serbanoiu (RuxandraDraws @ Fiverr)
Cover illustration: phanduy @ Fiverr

Ultimate World Publishing
Diamond Creek,
Victoria Australia 3089
www.writeabook.com.au

Testimonials

The first step in reducing stigma around alcohol and drug use is normalising conversations about our relationship with these substances. Tania has created a must-read guide for clinicians and service providers to assist in this process, packed full of techniques, strategies and practical guidance on how to work with clients wishing to address their alcohol or drug use. I recommend *Keep Calm and Treat Addiction* for anyone wanting to better understand evidence-based addiction treatment philosophy.

**Chris Raine,
Founder & CEO of Hello Sunday Morning**

Tania has written a very informative book on addiction and the associated behaviours incurred. The book is a wonderful resource for AOD practitioners and also for people wanting further knowledge and understanding in this field. It is clearly written, easy to understand and includes good examples throughout. Highly recommended.

**Josette Freeman,
Senior National Program Manager,
SMART Recovery Australia**

It is with pleasure that I endorse this book from my dear friend Tania. This practical guide is suitable for both clinicians, as well as people who have loved ones struggling with addiction. It is written in plain English without unnecessary jargon, which readers will appreciate and find easy to use – a wonderful resource to the addiction industry.

George Patriki,
Dual Diagnosis Consultant & Director of Gold Coast Addiction & Treatment Rehab

A beautifully written, concise, step-by-step approach that helps bridge a novice to an expert. Tania's easy to read, no-nonsense guide has given me the confidence to manage a difficult and complex aspect of GP practice, which is so easy to get wrong. A great go-to book that has found a permanent place on my desk.

Dr Kevin Naicker,
General Practitioner, Practice Principal of Michigan Drive Medical Practice (Gold Coast, Australia) & author of *My Mums My Foe*

This book is a valuable resource for all health professionals who work with people with addictions. Tania calls upon her own lengthy experience to offer words of wisdom and ever-so-practical advice for both novices entering this challenging and rewarding area of health practice and to those more experienced looking to 'brush-up' on their skills and knowledge. Tania's accessible and personable style makes the book easy to read and easy to re-read. I would highly recommend this 12-step guide to all health professionals who work with people with addictions.

**Associate Professor Julie Bradshaw,
RN, BHtlhSc, MNurs (Hons), PhD, SFHEA**

Keep Calm and Treat Addiction is a very insightful resource written for professionals and clinicians, which also holds valuable information for family and friends of people who use drugs. It is written clearly and provides an understanding of what both the patient and their loved ones endure. With valuable key points and professional advice, Tania's extensive experience and knowledge in addiction treatment – and passion to help others – shines through.

Personally, as the family member of someone who uses drugs, I found this book a unique and much sought after tool, full of excellent advice. I highly recommend it. I wish I had something like this years ago. Well done Tania!

Jenny Cook

Tania Kelly has written a great book that is factual and practical regarding alcohol and drug use, and of course treatment and assessment. Tania's many years of experience shines through this valuable resource. She manages to dispel myths about withdrawal and rehabilitation while she skilfully guides the reader through a need to know journey in the AODS field. I would recommend this book for professionals in the mental health and alcohol/drugs field. It is a great reference. Tania has managed to write a very readable book that is easy to navigate and contains chapters that the reader is likely to return to time and again.

Dr. Tonya Plumb,
Clinical and Forensic Psychologist

It's about time that such a user-friendly book was available.

As a social worker in a hospital, I frequently come across patients dealing with underlying addictions, many of them having been in a pattern for years. Too often they are put in the 'too-hard basket'. I regularly consult with Tania for practical advice and she has always helped me out. I have often wished I could just carry around her knowledge somehow – now I can thanks to *Keep Calm and Treat Addiction*! A must have for anyone working in this challenging area or anyone who has someone they know and need a bit of help to work out 'what do I do?'.

Margaret Barrett,
Senior Social Worker

A great read for new and seasoned clinicians. This really helped me to understand the many ways, I, as a clinician can support my clients through addiction; very easy to understand thanks to the real-world applications. I know that I can go to work and implement this tomorrow!

**Leishan Pace,
Founder, Director and
Principal Psychologist of Pace Ahead Psychology**

Wow! What a book… I've not read one like it on treating addiction. It is like being side by side learning from a skilled clinician's journey in helping those in need with addiction. This book is unique in teaching us the clinical skills – not in a technical and textbook way – but by a wonderful blend of the application of skills and knowledge within the actual real world that addiction specialists operate in. An invaluable resource for those wanting to learn specialist addiction skills.

**Garry Batt,
Counsellor, Dual Diagnosis Specialist, EMDR
Therapist, Credentialed Mental Health Nurse**

Experience in the field can't be faked, and here we have an opportunity to hear from someone with bucket loads of it. Sometimes, as we all know, experience equals burnout, so it's also refreshing to read Tania's insights and wisdoms come from a place of deep connection to the pain her clients suffer in the excruciating world of addiction. It's a complicated, messy, painful, frustrating, scary world to inhabit, and it takes support and knowledge and resources to manage it. If you want to offer your part in it all, read this book!

Janice Quadrio,
Mental Health Social Worker,
founder of The Ice Help Project, Mackay

As a clinician, I found this book easy to follow and feel I could apply this information to help clients. It's written in a way that could be easily understood by anyone who has an interest in supporting someone with addiction. I will certainly add this book to my toolkit.

Anne Oosterbroek,
Older Person's Mental Health Nurse Specialist

This information is useful, practical and relevant to workers across a range of discipline areas and work levels. I particularly liked the action points at the end of each chapter that remind the reader we don't work in 'silos' and that a holistic approach is needed when working with clients experiencing addiction. This resource is easy to read, and the personal anecdotes are invaluable. I would have loved a copy of this when working with young people with complex issues: AOD usually being one of these.

Great work Tania! I would also recommend your book to students studying human services courses as a very helpful resource to prepare them for work outside of academia.

Suewellyn Kelly,
Community Consultant and University Lecturer

As a social worker who is only starting out, I really appreciate the action points at the end of each chapter. They are clear and concise, and will help me build on my resources to help others in my everyday work life. As someone with English as a second language, although the book is full of information, the format makes it easy to read, with the material being broken down and explained in a way that is easily understood. Thanks Tania, this book is a great resource for all professionals working in caring professions.

Geyse Gomes,
Social Worker (new graduate)

Tania has drawn on her extensive clinical nursing experience, skills and knowledge to provide an evidence-based, easy to read resource for all health professionals. This book is an invaluable addition to any professional library.

**Rhonda Robinson,
Credentialed Mental Health Nurse**

Tania's *Keep Calm and Treat Addiction* is so aptly named. She shines welcome light on a field of work that, even for experienced clinicians, can be tempestuous and disheartening. Tania's experience is clearly evident – the countless difficult conversations she's had with people struggling through addiction and the heartbreaking family situations she has been confronted with make this book real, useful and compelling. And so does Tania's care and concern for these fellow human beings. She invites us to understand addiction from the perspective of the person and their family. From here, she can tackle the tough questions and give realistic suggestions for action. Tania's book is like having her in the room talking with you – it's down to earth, easy to understand, logical and reassuring. Experienced and new clinicians, all the people they support, and their families, will benefit greatly from the unique contribution Tania has made in understanding and treating addiction.

**Deb Rae,
Community Development Consultant,
MSocAdmin, GradDip HR&IR, BA & author of
*Getting There: Grief to Peace for Young Widows***

Dedication

To my clients who have taught me so much and given me the privilege of sharing in their recovery journeys.

To my husband Paul and my three children who love me unconditionally, always support me and believe in me, even when I have crazy ideas like writing a book.

Disclaimer

I have recreated conversations from my recollection of experiences over time. Names and characteristics have been changed.

Please note that alcohol is a drug too. Throughout this book, I use the terms substance, drug and alcohol interchangeably.

Contents

Testimonials 3
Dedication 11
Introduction 15

PART A: FUNDAMENTALS
Chapter 1: Expert **19**
Chapter 2: Urgency **31**
Chapter 3: Identity **41**
Chapter 4: Destiny **51**

PART B: POSSIBILITIES
Chapter 5: All or Nothing **65**
Chapter 6: Detox **73**
Chapter 7: Rehab **83**
Chapter 8: Rock Bottom **93**

PART C: JOURNEY
Chapter 9: Permission **107**
Chapter 10: Motivation **119**
Chapter 11: Power **131**
Chapter 12: Breakthrough **141**

Afterword 151
About the Author.. 153
Reference List 155
Offers 167

Introduction

Addiction is often put in the too-hard basket by clinicians. However, the right tools will give you the confidence you need to support the recovery of your clients. This book has been written as an accessible guide to help anyone who works with clients who use alcohol or other drugs, including psychologists, social workers, nurses, doctors, allied health professionals, counsellors, youth workers and caseworkers to name a few. Any clinicians who are new to addiction treatment services will also find this a valuable resource to assist them in their orientation and induction.

As you journey through the 12 steps found within, you will develop a deep understanding of the fundamentals of addiction treatment without having to invest a lot of time, energy or money into resources and training. Ideally, I recommend you read the complete book as it will provide a comprehensive overview of addiction treatment and recovery, giving you the tools you need to support your clients. From there, use it as a quick reference guide, so you can easily return to chapters of interest when you need that information in practice.

I love sharing concepts of alcohol and other drug treatment with clinicians, as in my experience, most clinicians embrace the knowledge and skills to support their clients with addiction. I make it my mission to normalise addictive behaviours, to reduce the stigma and ultimately improve the care provided to people struggling in their recovery journey. I didn't always work in the addiction field, and I know as a generalist clinician, it is hard to dedicate time to learning how to treat and support clients with every issue imaginable.

Whilst addiction treatment is a specialty area, there are many clients who won't visit an alcohol and drug service but are seeing a variety of other service providers. I saw there was a demand for an easy to read resource to support clinicians and service providers to work with their clients who are experiencing addiction. My goal is to demystify addiction, facilitating clinicians to grasp the fundamentals of addiction treatment and better support clients on their recovery journey.

So – are you ready to keep calm and treat addiction?

PART A

FUNDAMENTALS

The chains of habit are too weak to be felt until they are too strong to be broken.
                                            Samuel Johnson

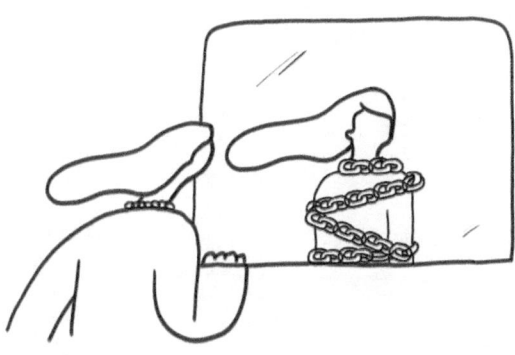

CHAPTER 1

Expert

Before you can break out of a prison you must realise that you are locked up.

Unknown

Self-doubt often holds clinicians back from working with their clients experiencing addiction. Many clinicians believe that being an expert in drugs and alcohol is required in order to help their clients. Repeatedly, I work with people who consider themselves inadequate, holding to the belief that addiction treatment is so complicated and specialised that they can't do it. But guess what? You don't have to be an expert in drugs to be able to work with your client to address their addiction. It's not a requirement that you have used drugs yourself and

Keep Calm and Treat Addiction

had a problem with drugs to be considered suitable to support someone with that challenge. At this very moment, you are the right person to work with your client. Do you want to know why?

You already have a desire to support your clients holistically, inclusive of their addiction, proof of this being that you are reading this book! The client has come to you as you have expertise they value. There's a reason that the client has chosen to work with you. They've selected you – they have trust in you, they've reached out and shared their struggle. You've succeeded in creating a therapeutic alliance.

People who use drugs, and their families, experience stigma in the community. The Australian Drug Foundation (ADF) recognises that many of the population see people experiencing addiction to blame for their circumstances[1]. There's a lot of stigma around drug use, making it extremely courageous of the client to confide in you. It was possibly really frightening for them. If your first instinct is to identify that the client needs to speak to a different clinician about their substance use, you risk reinforcing the stigma of addiction. You are likely to be already working with the client to address other aspects of their life. These could include relationship issues, financial concerns, past trauma in their lives, physical health issues and mental health challenges. Substance use is simply another factor in their lives that you can explore with them, as you collaboratively identify goals for a meaningful, rich life.

If your client mentions drug use and you immediately react by referring them to somebody else, an 'expert' whom you think is better suited, the chances are they won't follow through with

Expert

that referral and potentially they won't even come back and see you again. By working with your client, you keep your client engaged, and on the path of their recovery journey. Likewise, purely from a business standpoint, you're not sending your business elsewhere and losing clients to follow-up.

It is well established that, no matter the modality or frequency of the approach with your client, no matter your expertise in the therapy that you're delivering, despite your knowledge of drugs, client engagement is the single best predictor of outcome and creates the environment where change is possible[2]. Your skill in therapeutic alliance defines how successful your treatment is going to be, as well as the client's potential for change.

I found this a great comfort when I was starting out working in addiction treatment, when I felt inadequate and was concerned about failing my clients. I acknowledged I still had so much to learn at this early stage of my career, and I didn't want to do my clients a disservice being stuck with me! However, it has been my experience (and the research supports this) that just by sitting and listening to my client, showing empathy, being curious, helping them to feel comfortable talking to me and working through their issues is often enough – and without this, all the expert addiction knowledge in the world is rendered effectively useless anyway!

What is the cost of you feeling as though you need to be an expert? Of you reacting by referring your client on, as soon as they mention substance use? Most probably the client will relinquish addressing the issue and stop engaging. It's a missed opportunity. It may be some time before the client has the courage to raise their drug use with another clinician. I'm not implying that it's never the right time to refer a client on to specialist services. Conversely, there are times when this is recommended, and we will explore this in the coming chapters. However, the mere mention of drug use doesn't necessarily mean referral is required. Take solace in the revelation that you don't need to be the expert! Allowing the client to assume their rightful position as expert is client-centred care and it's well established that client-centred care is the desirable way to support recovery resulting in better outcomes[3].

So, you're sitting with your client; they've disclosed some drug use and you're unsure of what to do next. In this chapter I'm going to share with you a few ways to explore their addiction, enabling you to work together on their recovery plan.

Past victories

Chances are that your client has stopped or reduced their drug use in the past and has been successful doing it. This is a key area to explore, and a good place to start the discussion. Talk to them about what they did and the first steps that they took at that time.

Some helpful exploration questions include:

- What was happening in your life when you quit last time?
- What was different in your life back then compared to now?

Expert

- Can you replicate what worked for you in the past? (An example of this could be environment. Were they living in a more supportive environment back then to now, is there any way they can improve or change their current environment?)
- Was there a support group you accessed in the past that assisted your change? Would you be interested in accessing it again?
- What other strategies were helpful?

It is common when your client recalls past interventions that were conducive to change, they conclude that implementing these will make a difference in their current situation. On top of this, you should also find out if there were any obstacles, roadblocks or other things that got in their way last time that they may need to deal with. Explore these together and identify ways they can minimise the impact these barriers might have while they're trying to make changes today. The best consultations are ones with a spirit of collaboration, rather than with the focus of diagnosing and treating.

It is surprising how resourceful people can be when we explore their past victories. Strengths-based practice is an important foundation of alcohol and other drug practice[4]. An example is one of my previous clients, Jack, who successfully ceased cannabis, with little or no intervention from others. Jack just decided that enough was enough, and gave up, seemingly overnight! However, at a presentation five years later, Jack was homeless, working on stabilising accommodation and wanting to cease cannabis use again after he relapsed 12 months previously.

By examining his past abstinence, Jack identified that:

- when he was successful in the past, he had stable accommodation
- having a stable place to live is an important factor in his ability to cease his cannabis use
- he needs to first address his accommodation issues and will return to the goal of ceasing his cannabis at a future date.

In my experience the client often comes up with goals not directly related to their drug use. However, by addressing these issues and working on them, the client can position themselves for success in moderating or stopping their drug altogether.

What lies beneath

Consideration of the underlying causes of the drug use is important. Explore if the client is using substances to:

- deal with past trauma
- manage anxiety or other mental health issues.

I commonly see clients smoking cannabis to deal with their anxiety or drinking alcohol to feel confident in social situations. If the drug taking is merely a symptom of the real problem, and focus is exclusively on strategies to change the drug use, it can be compared to putting a plug in a volcano. The lava will be stemmed for the moment, however underneath, in the core of the volcano, all that lava is building up and the strategies aren't going to hold. That volcano is brewing, and the lava is all going to spill out again in no time, and possibly with a lot more intensity.

Of utmost importance is consideration of causal factors or underlying issues and how the client can be supported to deal with these or establish alternative ways of coping that are not substance related. Often, the drug is the one strategy that's worked for the client in dealing with their trauma or mental health issues. When taken away without alternative strategies, it leaves the client vulnerable and sets them up for negative outcomes.

> *Avoidance is a simple way of coping by not having to cope.*
> Lori Gottlieb

Potential risk

A common concern is the risk to the client when withdrawing from substances. Is it dangerous for them to stop 'cold turkey'? It is best practice for the client to engage with a general practitioner, for discussion and review regarding ceasing or reducing their substance use prior to instigating the plan. However, the client does not always adhere to best practice, and may decide on their own to suddenly stop or reduce their drug.

If a client is expressing to you that they wish to stop their substance without gradually reducing, it is important to first establish the following:

- Is the client experiencing dependence on the drug?
- Is the client experiencing dependence on more than one drug?

- Have they experienced withdrawal symptoms in the past when they have tried to stop?
- Do they live alone and have no access to a support person who can stay with them?
- Do they have other significant medical or psychiatric comorbidities[5]?

If the client answers yes to one or more of the above, it is recommended they consult their general practitioner, and possibly an alcohol and drug service for a comprehensive assessment to ensure they are kept safe in their withdrawal. This process can be supported by phoning an alcohol and other drug (AOD) service to ask for advice over the phone, hence reassuring the client that you are here to support them, and to ensure they are kept safe and well. Withdrawal will be discussed in more detail in Chapter 6. If your client is using drugs and pregnant, it is advised for them to see a specialist alcohol and drug service as soon as possible. Remember, if ever in doubt, seek medical advice.

Application

You might be thinking, I've had clients in the past who can't remember a time that they didn't use drugs, hence can't explore any times that they've been successful in cutting down or stopping their substance. It's important to refrain from taking the role of the expert and coming up with all of the answers for the client because evidence shows that just doesn't work and it's not going to be successful for the client. If they can't recall previous reduction or cessation of their drug, try exploring other substances they have ceased or reduced.

Expert

An example of this is clients I've worked with who are using methamphetamine, and have never been able to change their use, but have quit cigarettes, successfully without any support whatsoever. This past success of conquering nicotine addiction is a great resource to tap into because the client has shown tremendous strength in overcoming this dependency. Exploration of strategies implemented to quit smoking are often transferrable to changing behaviour around other addictive substances.

An example might be that one of the first things the client did when quitting cigarettes was to distance themselves from their smoking friends for a period of time. Can they replicate this now in relation to their methamphetamine use? And just like they avoided the tobacco counter, are there ways they can distance themselves from their methamphetamine supply such as getting rid of dealer contacts in their phone, taking themselves off social media or changing their phone number altogether? Although the drugs are very different, often strategies for behaviour change are common to all substances and easily adapted.

Many clinicians are concerned also that because they themselves have never used drugs, that they will appear as unauthentic. This is a fear that I had in the early days of my AOD practice, afraid that clients would see me as a fraud and not the right person to be working with because I hadn't experienced illicit drug use for myself. I can recall one such experience when I was facilitating a group. One of the participants said, 'Look at you. You wouldn't have a clue. You haven't done what we've done and there's no possible way you could offer anything of value to us.'

Keep Calm and Treat Addiction

I expressed to the group my agreeance, that lived experience workers are valued in our line of work, and that area of opportunity is growing in health. I encourage all my clients if that's an area they feel passionate about, to research courses they can complete to work towards a career in addiction support, as lived experience workers are difficult to find. I didn't need to prove anything to the group or disagree with the client. I simply reassured the group I was doing my best to support them with the skills and knowledge I had developed.

You may feel concerned that you aren't equipped to assess their risk. There are a selection of screening tools, measures and scales that are helpful in determining risk. As a bonus gift, I have compiled a members-only webpage with downloads and links to evidence-based tools to use in your practice, along with many other worksheets discussed throughout this book. I keep this page updated with new resources and tools as they become available, including links to free AOD training. If you would like access to this page, please email tania@taniakellyhealth.com.au and request your password to this valuable resource. This and other special offers are listed at the back of this book.

Expert

ACTION POINTS

- Compile a resource folder of AOD related resources to support your clients (AOD toolbox).

- Practise utilising these AOD tools in clinical supervision.

- Want to dig deeper? Engage in online learning to upskill in AOD knowledge.

CHAPTER 2

Urgency

The journey in between what you once were and who you are now becoming is where the dance of life takes place.
                                                    Barbara De Angelis

Families often drive the urgency of the presenting situation, putting pressure on service providers. They can be compelled by desperation, and feel if everyone doesn't jump to attention now, the opportunity will be lost to rescue their loved one from the drug and the damage it has caused. Sometimes the pressure comes from the client. There can be catastrophic thinking, and the belief that if the clinician isn't available to help them right this minute, they will never recover.

Keep Calm and Treat Addiction

This concept of urgency is a foundational misconception that I really hope to provide clarity about for all service providers and clinicians. Pressure and urgency are challenges that I deal with daily from clients, family members and other service providers. It is of vital importance, as a clinician, not to be drawn into the drama of urgency projected by others, to ensure you remain rational and level-headed. It is so easy to be unknowingly drawn into urgency (I have done it many times) and the emotion that surrounds it.

There are lots of reasons to not get drawn into urgency. It's important to ensure that all goals set are client centred. Leaping into action driven by urgency doesn't allow time to explore with the client their current situation and what's most important to them. Often, when there is a real sense of urgency, it's because the client is being driven by a crisis, and it's the crisis that's the real issue. The client is not necessarily ready to address their drug use, despite it appearing this way on the surface. Once the crisis settles down, what often happens then is the client is nowhere to be found. Their goal was primarily to manage the crisis, and once the crisis passes, they return to their drug use and disengage with treatment.

Not being driven by urgency and instead taking the time to explore the situation with the client, gives room to explore their values and goals. This approach enables the right intervention to be chosen for the client, rather than being reactive. Families and friends are often understandably exhausted and want someone to 'fix' the situation, a magic wand. The client may be simply appeasing them by coming along to see you, and on the surface say all the things their family wants to hear.

Urgency

Although there is pressure to rescue the client, not reacting to urgency allows the whole recovery journey to be considered, not just the crisis. Operating in crisis and urgency mode also contributes to burnout. It's exhausting. So, by not feeding into urgency, you're going to avoid burnout for yourself, and burnout for the family. Ultimately, by not buying into urgency, and ensuring that the right interventions are chosen for the client, the client will experience better outcomes. This methodology results in client empowerment, not client rescue. By exploring and working through a plan with the client, they are empowered to rescue themselves.

You might be surprised to know that in studies of people who have received treatment for alcohol disorders in the United States, between a quarter and a half of them relapse in the first year[1]. Relapse is common, and in fact studies show 40–60% of people in treatment relapse at least once[2]. There are no quick fixes for addiction, and as the statistics suggest, there are going to be ups and downs and forks in the road.

However, don't let these statistics make your feel despondent! If the client is engaged with you in a therapeutic alliance, if they are the ones who have arrived at their treatment option, then they're more likely to commit to it. If you allow yourself to be driven by the urgency of the client, or the urgency of the family, the client most likely has not made an informed choice of their treatment plans and options and is unlikely to stick to the path for long. This results in further erosion of their self-esteem, setting unrealistic expectations, thereby further fracturing relationships with their friends and family. Furthermore, the client and the family can waste a lot of time and money. It's important that time is taken for education and discussion to enable both the client and the family to understand the recovery process and identify realistic expectations.

I regularly meet with family members who state, 'We have to act now. My son or my daughter has finally identified that there's an issue, and we need to get them into rehab today before they change their mind'. This belief potentially comes about as a result of television programs like *Dr Phil*, where the young person is dragged into the show and Dr Phil works his magic and convinces the young person to agree to treatment. His workers swoop in and transport the young person to the ranch immediately. In a perfect world with unlimited resources and money, this scenario could maybe be possible. Reality, unfortunately, looks very different. We also aren't privy to the outcomes after the camera turns off, to see how long the young person stays in the rehab facility.

Slow down

The key is to slow the process down and ease the pressure of urgency, which isn't easy when you've got a lot of heightened emotions and expectations. The problem of drug use, the issue of addiction has likely been in that person's life for a long time. It's better to take the time to explore and ensure that the right path is chosen by the client, maximising opportunity for positive outcomes.

You're probably thinking, that's easier said than done! When somebody comes for a consult ready for immediate action, and the family is insisting on it, what am I supposed to do? I agree, this isn't an easy situation. Firstly, work with the client and their

Urgency

family to gain some perspective. Assist them to identify the longevity of the problem, stressing the importance of ascertaining the best course of action. Facilitating an understanding of the cycle of addiction is important however the family may be resistant to accepting that lapses and relapses are part of the cycle.

High distress intolerance is common amongst clients who use substances[3]. Substances have provided an instant relief to their circumstances; therefore, it is not surprising that they are now seeking urgent resolve to their situation. Likewise, elevated distress intolerance influences unfavourable outcomes in addiction treatment, and can even increase withdrawal symptoms[4]. Guiding the client in some mindfulness-based activities to reduce distress intolerance is an effective intervention to introduce at this time to strengthen reduction of drug use and relapse[5]. It is important that we are not feeding into the client's need to have their distress immediately resolved, but rather, model and teach ways to sit with distress and discover alternative strategies to cope.

Empower the client to rescue themselves.
                                                        Tania Kelly

Crisis management

In crisis presentations, draw attention to addressing the crisis. A common predicament is a relationship breakdown. Take Anna for example, who has been given an ultimatum by her partner: stop drinking or the relationship is over. Naturally, Anna presents with a sense of urgency and panic, distraught at the thought of her relationship ending.

Keep Calm and Treat Addiction

A helpful focus in this situation is exploration of ways Anna can protect her relationship while she works on her alcohol use. Maybe this involves Anna finding alternative accommodation for a period of time, staying with extended family or friends. If there was a quick fix way to address Anna's addiction, I'd be rich by now! Unfortunately, there isn't – addiction treatment requires time and a lot of energy. Sustained change will not happen overnight, and substance use cannot be solved urgently.

Often the client is dealing with natural consequences of their drug use, such as impending court dates. Maybe the client has failed a drug test at work, and they are under pressure to resolve the issue, or face losing their employment. These are opportunities to elicit change, and it is beneficial to adequately explore all aspects of the client's life being impacted by their substance use. The clinician can activate the motivation for change by simply being curious and reflecting the client's account of their circumstances. The client is likely to want to accelerate towards concluding the treatment and reception of a letter of support. Don't underestimate the power of motivational interviewing in these circumstances even though the client appears only focused on escaping their circumstances.

Family support

Family and supportive others (when they are available) are a key component of the client's support system and recovery plan. It is important to ensure they are supported and (if possible) educated to understand how to best support their loved one. If your service does not have the capability to support the family as well as the client, there are other services that can offer

Urgency

this. Evidence suggests that family-centred therapy improved outcomes in AOD treatment[6].

In my experience, it is typically helpful to work with the client without their family members present. Meeting with the individual gives them space for honesty, as they can often conceal and suppress out of concern for their family members. When working with clients and their families, I frequently suggest we start the session together so everyone can share their perception of the week passed, and then the body of the consult is spent individually with the client. Once the body of the session is complete, I discuss with the client what information and feedback we are going to provide to their family, and the consultation is concluded with a family discussion of the outcomes and plan for the week ahead.

Application

What about the families and clients who are angry when their expectations aren't met? They will only be appeased by immediate attention to their demands. I've experienced ultimatums, declaring that my inaction is causing the client to just go out and use again, and it is all my fault. As distressing as this can be for clinicians, it's important not to get caught up in the emotion and be reactive in these situations. Emphasise to the client and family that we can only work with the resources available to us and provide both the client and family with some tools and strategies they can utilise in the meantime while they are waiting for their appointment or booking.

Keep Calm and Treat Addiction

When threatened by media attention, I encourage it! I have urged many an angry family member and client to talk to their local member of parliament and voice their frustrations at the lack of AOD resources and treatment. I agree with them and reassure that we as service providers get frustrated too, and one way to evoke change is by raising awareness of community needs. The more complaints that are raised, the more likely we are to see an increase in resources.

If there is a delay between the client seeking intervention and receiving treatment, it's important to have a safety plan in place. This is similar to developing a mental health safety plan. Consider the supports that the client may be able to access out of hours, such as AOD telephone counselling and emergency mental health numbers. Reassure the client and family that they can call an ambulance or present to the emergency department should they need to.

Urgency

ACTION POINTS

- Compile a list of services providing support to families experiencing addiction and add it to your AOD toolbox.

- Put together mindfulness resources that can be provided to your clients.

- Explore therapeutic interventions specific to reducing distress intolerance, practise them in supervision.

CHAPTER 3

Identity

What lies behind us and what lies before us are tiny matters compared to what lies within us.

Ralph Waldo Emerson

Commonly, clients are labelled as alcoholics, drug addicts or drug abusers. Sometimes clients define themselves using these classifications. However, in my practice I prefer not to use these labels. You may feel comfortable with this terminology and question why I consider these descriptions as unconstructive in the recovery process. Many of us have become accustomed to the categories alcoholic, addict and abuser being applied to our clients consistently amongst both the community and the health sector.

Keep Calm and Treat Addiction

In my experience, by avoiding these labels, we're choosing not to define the client's identity by a single behaviour. The terms alcoholic and addict conjure stereotypical images of people who are not valued by society. A client-centred recovery model utilises language that is reflective of ethical principles, indicative of diagnostic language[1]. The client's drug taking behaviour does not define who they are; holistically we consider the social, spiritual, mental and physical health when assessing a client. Just as we don't expect a person with diabetes or asthma to be defined by their illness, nor should we for a person with a substance use disorder.

Using stigmatising language can subconsciously affect the attitude of care givers toward their clients[2]. A person described as having a substance use disorder reflects a client who has a condition requiring treatment. In contrast, labelling someone as a substance abuser suggests that it is the person causing the condition. By using non-stigmatising terminology reflective of diagnostic language, we are creating hope and focusing on future potential. The presence of hope is directly related to recovery from substance use and considered a protective factor[3]. Utilising stigmatising language suggesting that there is no hope for recovery is not evidence-based practice. A link to a free resource exploring stigmatising language and providing recovery-focused alternatives can be accessed on my members-only webpage (see Offer 1 at the back of this book).

By refraining from referring to the client as an alcoholic or addict, we are focused on supporting the client to explore all the other aspects of themselves, building their identity separate to substance use. If they do have a substance use diagnosis, it is suggestive of a treatable condition that does not need to define them.

Identity

You may be surprised to know that one in four Australians are drinking alcohol at risky levels and 10–15% of emergency department presentations are alcohol related according to Australia's national alcohol strategy[4]. Think about the people around you – your friends, family, work colleagues. Would you consider one out of four of the people you know an alcoholic? I think that your answer would be most certainly not! Have you considered, that by labelling substance users as alcoholics or addicts, we are creating a false sense of security for the rest of the population who are drinking alcohol at risky levels?

If ourselves and those around us don't look like the alcoholic or addict stereotype, then it's probably concluded that there isn't a problem. In my experience, that's often not the case. There's a huge range of drug and alcohol use that absolutely needs to be addressed, not just the extreme end of the spectrum.

How do we explore a person's substance use and discover if it is congruent with their values and goals, without judgement? In this chapter, we're going to look at three ways this can be achieved, without emphasising stigma or labelling the client.

Miracle question

Firstly, let's consider a simple intervention called the miracle question. The miracle question is an example of an intervention of solution-focused therapy, whereby the client identifies their desired life[5]. This tool is particularly helpful when your client can't see a life without their substance use. Likewise, it is useful in helping the client recognise that their substance use is blocking their fulfilment of values and goals.

Keep Calm and Treat Addiction

Present the miracle question in a simple way, such as:

Imagine that tonight, while you are asleep, a miracle takes place. When you wake up in the morning, all your problems have been resolved and your life is exactly how you would like it to be.

Once the client has had some time to think, these questions are helpful for further exploration:

- What's the first thing you notice when you wake up?
- What are some of the things you observe, that tells you your life has improved?
- Describe what things have changed.
- What will your friends notice has changed in your life?
- How would you spend your day?
- What are you thinking, feeling?

The client may, or may not, identify if they are using substances in their preferred life. If they haven't mentioned substance use, you may consider gently probing if they see their drug use as part of their new life. Once there has been ample consideration of the new life, explore what the client could do to help themselves move in some small way toward the world they have described.

Take my client Mary for example. Mary has recently had her children removed from her care and is smoking methamphetamine. When asked the miracle question, Mary sees herself in stable accommodation, living with her children. She feels happy and her family notice she is calmer and she is taking her children to

Identity

and from school. Mary spends her evenings helping the kids with their homework and watching her favourite show on television. Mary identifies that she is no longer using methamphetamine and isn't hanging out with her usual friends. When considering what her first step towards this ideal life is, Mary concludes that she is going to get off social media and block the phone numbers of her associates that she smokes methamphetamine with.

Looking forward, looking back

This intervention is indicated if the client has had a decline in their quality of life as a result of using substances, however, they may be having difficulty acknowledging this. For clients who have deteriorating health such as liver disease due to alcohol use, this is a helpful strategy. Have the client think back to a time, such as five years ago.

Facilitate consideration of the following:

- What does your life look like?
- Describe your relationships
- How were you feeling about yourself?
- What did an average day entail for you?
- Were you using drugs, how often, in what quantity?
- How was your health?

Once this has been explored, the focus is diverted to five years into the future. Explore the same questions, on the basis that the client will continue to do what they are doing currently. Possibly the client will recognise that their quality of life will continue to decline as it has over the past five years should they continue with their current behaviours. For some of my clients, this has been a very sombre moment, when faced with the reality that they will most likely be dead in five years if they continue their substance use. For others, the reality that their children will be five years older, and still not in their care is a solemn reminder of the consequences of continued drug use.

Finish on the consideration of their future should they stop or reduce their substance use. What does five years down the track look like then? This concludes the discussion with hope, an essential element of addiction recovery[6]. Once again, assist the client to identify one small change they could implement in the week ahead to move them closer to this reality. Like the miracle question, this tool is solutions focused.

Micro counselling skills

Good old-fashioned core counselling skills create an environment conducive to exploring substance use. These skills encompass:

- rapport building
- active listening
- summarising
- minimal encouragers
- reflection of both feeling and content
- reframing
- open questions[7].

Whilst having a conversation with the client, utilising micro counselling skills, we are also urged to do so with a spirit of

Identity

motivational interviewing. Reflecting on the client's strengths and expressing belief in them are important in creating a safe environment where the client relaxes and shares with you without the fear of judgement[8].

Application

I recall one miracle question experience that caught me off guard and thinking on my feet! When I asked 18-year-old Stacey the miracle question, she beamed with delight. She confidently described her ideal life on a deserted island, on her own, in a cottage where no-one would bother her, and she would have… an endless supply of weed!!! More weed than she could ever smoke!!! Now you might be thinking, how on earth do I frame that miracle question in a way that supports recovery?

No matter what miracle the client conjures up, it can still be utilised to explore recovery. Obviously, an endless supply of weed wasn't the miracle I was hoping to work with. However, we went on to explore the feelings behind this hydroponic heaven. Stacey explained she was feeling relaxed, her anxiety was gone. She recognised that there was no-one hassling her or telling her what to do. Stacey chose the beach, a place where she feels most at peace. Lastly, she chose solitude, not a room full of her friends to smoke and party with.

By exploring the context of her miracle, we were able to discover the following about Stacey:

- Stacey values solitude
- Stacey wants to be free from anxiety

Keep Calm and Treat Addiction

- The beach is a place where Stacey feels peaceful
- Stacey wants to make her own choices and not have people tell her what to do.

You might be thinking, what next after the miracle question or looking forward, looking back? How do I utilise the outcomes of these tools? Stacey has identified some values including solitude and peace. Often our clients have never explored their values, and what is important to them. In my practice, I adopt Dialectical Behaviour Therapy (DBT) and Acceptance and Commitment Therapy (ACT) constructs, both evidence-based modalities for substance use disorder[9]. Identifying values, the direction in which the client wants to move, provides a roadmap for life, rather than just short-term goals. Values cards can be utilised to explore the various areas in your client's life, and what is important to them. Once values are identified, all goals defined can be evaluated to check that they are congruent with the client's values. Values are also helpful when the client needs to plan and make decisions. For example, Stacey might be deciding whether to pursue a relationship with an ex-partner, who was verbally abusive to her in the past. When Stacey considers her value of having a peaceful life, she determines that entering this relationship is not going to support her value and she decides against it.

What about the client who refers to themselves as an alcoholic, addict or drug abuser? I have worked with many clients who define themselves this way and consider this label a vital component of their recovery. Many find solace in the framework of Alcoholics Anonymous (AA), and the social identity gained by membership supports their recovery[10]. If assuming this identity is working for the client, it is the right philosophy for

Identity

them. Many residential rehabilitation programs align with the AA abstinence model. Nevertheless, when reflecting or summarising in counselling sessions, I model the use of non-stigmatising language to ensure I am not reinforcing potentially harmful self-construct.

What you do doesn't define who you are.
Tania Kelly

Keep Calm and Treat Addiction

ACTION POINTS

- Include miracle question and looking forward worksheets in your AOD toolbox.

- Explore Acceptance & Commitment Therapy and Dialectical Behaviour Therapy if you are not familiar with them. Add some values cards to your resources.

- Have available contact numbers for Alcoholics and Narcotics Anonymous should your client value this support system.

CHAPTER 4

Destiny

The great thing in this world is not so much where you stand, as in what direction you are moving.

Oliver Wendell Holmes

It is often assumed, if a person is experimenting with drugs, they're destined to develop a full-blown addiction. Substance use presents in many forms, ranging from experimental use to dependent drug use. I've consulted with many concerned parents over the years who upon finding some cannabis in their teenager's room, have visions of them being on the street, injecting methamphetamine, doomed to be dependent on drugs forever. It's important to remember that this isn't necessarily the case. Some families (and clinicians) are very naïve to drug use and are basing their assumptions on sensationalised images from the media or movies. Understandably, their mind goes crazy with concern for their teenager.

Don't assume the worst when a client reveals that they're using a drug. It's important not to catastrophise and allow our own beliefs and values about drug use to cloud our reaction. Instead allow space for curiosity in conversation and exploration of the situation with your client. It generally takes repeated use of a drug over a period of time to develop dependence; a person won't necessarily become dependent after using a substance a few times.

Overreacting and instilling fear further marginalises people. Media often sensationalise their reporting on drug use with fear-evoking language and images that arouse panic. An obvious example of this is the HIV prevention campaign in the 1980s; remember the grim reaper? There is great debate about whether fear campaigns achieve their desired result. However, one thing is certain about fear driven campaigns; they further marginalise and stigmatise a population that is already vulnerable[1].

Ice (methamphetamine) users are often portrayed as violent, psychotic and 'hooked' from the first experience of the drug. However, the reality is that this represents 25% of users at the extreme end of the spectrum of methamphetamine use[2]. Unfortunately, the other 75% of users when exposed to this form of media then switch off, believing that all the warnings they hear about methamphetamine are lies, as they are not currently experiencing these symptoms. I have experienced firsthand my clients telling me this, lulled into a false sense of security that they are somehow immune to the effects of the drug. This is sadly untrue, and I have often witnessed the steady decline of these clients due to their complacency.

By not overreacting to the client's drug use, the clinician is able to give unconditional positive regard regardless of what the client is revealing. In contrast to the judgement and emotion the client often faces at home, you provide a safe space where they are free to be honest and transparent without fear of retribution.

The 2016 National Drug Strategy Household Survey reports that 3.1 million Australians acknowledged using an illicit (illegal) drug in the preceding 12 months[3]. That's a lot of people using drugs who are not living on the streets or attacking nurses in emergency departments. This demonstrates that using a drug doesn't always equate to dependence or problematic behaviour.

As a clinician, if we choose to adopt fear-based interventions in the hope of encouraging change, we destroy any chance of building a therapeutic alliance. This creates a barrier to treatment, the client perceiving that you are out of touch and unable to help them.

Let's now take a closer look at reasons people use drugs, and the spectrum of substance use. This chapter will also examine dependence and tolerance and why these are important considerations in treatment of substance use.

Keep Calm and Treat Addiction

What's the hype?

The fact is humankind have been using drugs for a long time. Did you know that:

- prior to 1903 Coca-Cola contained cocaine, not caffeine
- alcohol dates back to 3500 BC
- tobacco was introduced to Europe in 1493
- cannabis was introduced to France in 1800
- in 1946 there was an estimated 40,000,000 opium smokers in China[4].

When working with people who use substances, I am provided with lots of reasons why they choose to do drugs. These are some of the reasons I have heard, I am sure there are many more!

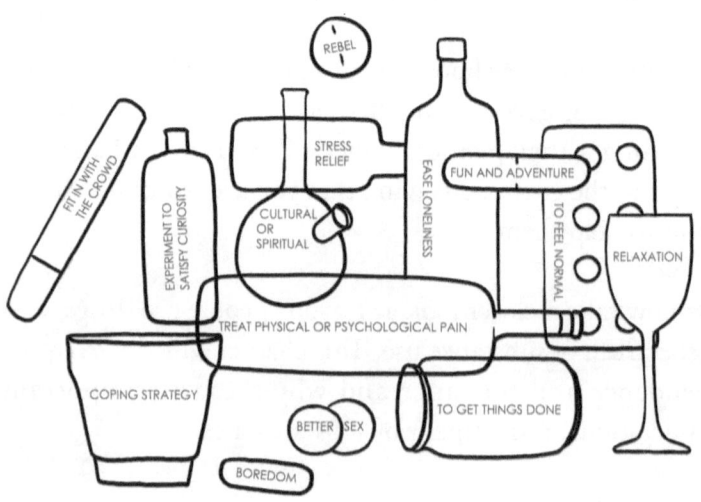

Destiny

What I have learnt is that people are using drugs because the effects of the drug provides a benefit for them. Their choice of drug is often influenced by its availability and cost. People also can have different experiences of drug taking depending on their emotions and environment at the time. For example, if someone is drinking alcohol because of a relationship breakdown, the effects of the drug in comparison to drinking because they have received a job promotion are not the same. Likewise, someone smoking cannabis with friends can behave differently to when they are smoking it in isolation at home.

The spectrum

It is helpful to consider drug use across a spectrum, considering the various classifications of drug use[5]. This ensures we stay realistic and non-sensational about our client's drug use. Drugs generally are not instantly addictive and attempting to frighten people into quitting or not experimenting by warning that using it once and you're changed forever, is simply not true for everyone.

At one end of the spectrum we have non-use or abstinence, and at the other dependence. Between these two extremes are experimental, occasional and regular use. Remember, the spectrum is not a continuum; people can move both ways along the spectrum. Furthermore, being in one stage doesn't necessarily indicate movement to the next. Some people will never move from the stage they are currently in.

Keep Calm and Treat Addiction

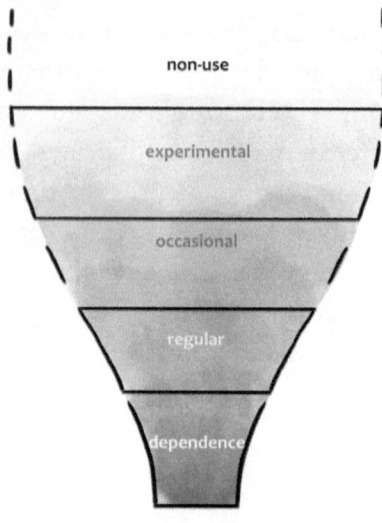

Spectrum of drug use

Consider adolescents; experimental use is most common. In the absence of past trauma, many young people are looking for adventure, pushing the boundaries, hungry for excitement. A young person who chooses to try a pill at a music festival won't necessarily go on to develop a dependence on ecstasy or any other drug. As a matter of fact, they may dislike the experience, and never use drugs again!

I have worked with many clients who use occasionally; it may be for social reasons or on special occasions. This can be true for clients who work in a fly-in-fly-out or drive-in-drive-out lifestyle, where residence is at the worksite for a length of time, until the return home for a week off. In this situation, the client often can remain substance free whilst at work because the environment demands it, however the minute they return home the drug use begins. They can stop their drug use in time to ensure a clear drug screen upon return to the worksite.

Destiny

Although some people use occasionally and never change from this pattern of use, many find that over time or at different periods in their lives, their use becomes more regular. Take my client Bill for example. Bill worked his entire life for a company and enjoyed returning home Friday afternoons to share a bottle of wine with his wife June, in celebration of the long-awaited weekend. For over forty years, Bill had never experienced any concerns about his level of use. Upon retirement, Bill's wife continued in her employment, and Bill found himself home alone, feeling a bit lost by the change in routine and purpose. He found himself opening a bottle of red at lunch time and finishing it by mid-afternoon to hide his drinking from June. Despite maintaining occasional use for most of his life without a problem, Bill now finds himself regularly drinking and on the slippery slope of dependence and tolerance.

Addiction denied is recovery delayed.
Mokokoma Mokhonoana

Dependence and tolerance

Bill has moved from drinking four standard drinks once a week, to drinking a minimum of eight standard drinks every day. He finds that over time, he is not feeling as relaxed from his eight standard drinks and opens another bottle of wine in the evening when June gets home. This reduction in the effect of the drug, needing more to get the same effect, is known as tolerance. Tolerance to substances is a result of decreased sensitivity of the neurotransmitters in the brain[6]. Due to this adaptation of his neurotransmitters, Bill is likely to experience symptoms of physical withdrawal if he doesn't drink.

Keep Calm and Treat Addiction

Additionally, Bill has stopped playing golf on Thursday afternoons with his old work colleagues. June also notices that Bill takes his bottle of wine out to the shed and drinks alone, rather than watching the news with her as they have done for many years. If Bill doesn't have a bottle of wine in the house and his lunchtime drink is delayed, he finds himself feeling cranky and irritable until he makes the trip to the corner bottle-o to satisfy his craving. Bill also finds that if he has two bottles of wine in the house, he is likely to finish both over lunch, and sometimes starts even earlier than lunch. His GP has recently told him that his liver is not functioning normally as a result of his drinking, and he is likely to damage it permanently if he doesn't reduce or cut down, but this is not incentive enough for Bill to change his drinking. All the behaviours and signs that Bill is demonstrating are evidence of dependence. The more of these behaviours evident, the higher the level of dependence[6].

There are many screening and assessment tools for dependence available, the ASSIST (Alcohol, Smoking and Substance Involvement Screening Test), developed by the World Health Organisation (WHO), being my choice for clinicians. The ASSIST considers not just dependence, but risks from drug use right across the spectrum, for all types of substances. It provides the clinician with brief interventions to deliver to the client according to their level of risk[7]. For clients using only alcohol, the AUDIT (Alcohol Use Disorders Identification Test), also developed by the WHO, is a simple tool providing a great framework for brief intervention. A link to these can be accessed by requesting your bonus gift (see offers at back of this book). Diagnostical perspective can be gained by reviewing the *Diagnostic and Statistical Manual for Mental Disorders, Fifth*

Destiny

Edition (DSM-5), which outlines the criteria for diagnosing either alcohol or substance use disorder.

Application

You might be thinking, if a client is happy experimenting, or sticking with occasional use, what should I do? Consider having the client complete an ASSIST screening tool with you (if they agree), which will indicate the level of risk, and the brief interventions that are appropriate for that level of risk. What is most important is to ensure that both the client, and those around them are kept safe. Maintaining your relationship with the client, and keeping them engaged, means that you are available to them when they are ready for change.

At times, I have had families insisting that their young person, who is experimenting with occasional use, goes to a residential rehabilitation facility. These families are practising 'tough love', and putting ultimatums on the table such as, 'Stop using or there's the door!'. Likewise, these parents contact me asking about drug testing kits, planning to test their kids to prove whether they are using. In these instances, the family are highly emotive and concerned, clutching at strategies to try and gain control of the situation. As a clinician, it is important not to be judgemental and to express empathy for their situation. They are doing the best they can, with the knowledge they have. Nevertheless, I gently explore with the family the purpose of their strategies, and what outcomes they hope to achieve. We also consider the undesired outcomes that may occur, and what the consequences of these might be. For example, what might be the consequences of drug testing your child, and

Keep Calm and Treat Addiction

what impact will that have on your relationship? I emphasise the importance of maintaining trust and communication, and often the parents reach the conclusion that drug testing is not going to achieve an outcome that is helpful.

Remember that sometimes it is the right time to refer the client on. When in doubt, phone a specialist service for advice. If upon screening your client dependence is indicated, a specialist AOD service will be able to advise the best recovery treatment plan.

Destiny

ACTION POINTS

- Include the ASSIST and AUDIT in your AOD toolbox.

- Revise the DSM-5 and diagnostic criteria related to substance use should this be appropriate to your discipline.

- Network with your local AOD specialist service and learn about referral processes.

PART B

POSSIBILITIES

There are multiple pathways to addiction recovery, and ALL are cause for celebration!

William L. White

CHAPTER 5

All or Nothing

If one oversteps the bounds of moderation, the greatest pleasures cease to please.

Epictetus

Abstinence is often presented as the only option for clients who are experiencing problems associated with their drug use. Abstinence isn't the only answer and if this is presented, people can be deterred from help-seeking. It's important for abstinence to be presented as a choice, not the only solution, because setting realistic goals is crucial to supporting your client's success in moving forward with their recovery plan. Abstinence models can be intimidating for many; the thought of life without drugs is just unthinkable. When presented with abstinence as the only possibility, many are completely overwhelmed.

If you offer abstinence as an option rather than a requirement, your clients are more likely to engage in treatment. They may not be ready to consider abstinence but be prepared to talk about a lot of other issues in their life. Building a therapeutic relationship positions you to explore their substance use later when they're ready. The client needs to be in control of their recovery journey. For some, there will be myriad attempts at moderation before concluding that moderation isn't a viable option, and abstinence needs to be considered. It's important to remember that the client's recovery journey is a marathon, not a sprint. There are a lot of lessons to be learnt along the way, these strengthening the client's resilience to future obstacles.

If abstinence is to be considered, it also needs a plan. In some cases, it can be dangerous to pursue abstinence, and a plan needs to be developed to manage risk and ensure safety. Many people aren't aware that a person can die from alcohol or benzodiazepine withdrawal when stopping abruptly. If the client's level of dependence is high enough it puts them at risk of seizures and ultimately death. Abstinence is not a strategy to be considered without seeking medical advice, particularly for alcohol, benzodiazepines, GHB or ketamine[1]. Maintaining safety reinforces the need for planning so that the right interventions and supports are put in place.

Furthermore, when abstinence is compelled, it can reinforce the client's sense of hopelessness and failure when they are unable to maintain the abstinence. A slip-up can result in self-loathing and plummeting self-esteem. I have seen many occasions where the

All or Nothing

family insist upon abstinence, and a slip-up is seen as a complete failure. This has a devastating impact on both the confidence of the client, and family relationships. In this chapter we're going to explore abstinence, the circumstances when it is best considered, and how to prepare the client for abstinence.

Consultation

One of the first steps that's critical when planning for abstinence or any significant change in drug use is to engage with a GP for medical advice. A GP can ensure the relevant testing is completed and ensure that appropriate advice is given around reducing or cutting out the client's drug. This is particularly crucial regarding alcohol and benzodiazepines. In my experience, if a GP isn't confident regarding addiction, they will refer to a specialist drug and alcohol service to provide that additional support. Generally, there are minimal risks when ceasing most drugs outside of alcohol or benzodiazepines, however it is best to consult with a health professional who can consider the client's entire health, as the clinician may be unaware of additional physical conditions. Consultation with a GP is particularly advised when a screening for dependence has been completed, indicating moderate or high dependence/risk. On the other hand, if your client is on the lower end of dependence/risk, or if they're experimenting, consultation with a GP is generally not required. Nonetheless, engagement with a GP is always a good thing, especially if your client has not had a medical check for some time.

It can be argued that abstinence is easier than moderation. For some, completely cutting out a substance is less stressful than constantly moderating and measuring. Goals of moderation are focused on quality of life, rather than the absence of the drug, and have a harm minimisation philosophy. If a person has a physical dependence on a substance, it is my experience that moderation is unlikely to work for them. Likewise, if moderation has been unsuccessful in the past, it is doubtful that it will work now. Sometimes a combination plan that includes a period of abstinence, followed by a trial of moderation might be favoured by the client.

I have had many clients who decide to start their treatment with a three-month period of abstinence prior to moderating. Often upon nearing the end of their abstinence, the client is feeling so good that they decide it is too risky to return to moderation and continue with abstinence as a long-term plan. Others move on to moderation and quickly discover that the freedom they experienced in abstinence has been quickly replaced by stress and relapse. Trials of moderation and abstinence, accompanied by lapses and relapses, are often part of the recovery journey. Peer support groups with a harm minimisation philosophy such as SMART Recovery are a safe place for support for those clients who are moderating or abstaining.

Level of use

Before deciding on a plan forward, of vital importance is knowing how much the client is using. In my experience, many people are unaware of how much of their drug they are using, or exactly how many standard drinks they are consuming. Providing the client with a diary or an app that can adequately record what they're using over a period of a week or two is

All or Nothing

helpful in planning ahead for change. In fact, this tool alone frequently motivates the client to use less by being mindful of how much they're using. A diary can also be effective in identifying high risk times of the day and emotional or external triggers to substance use.

In Australia, alcohol is measured in standard drinks, which is equivalent to 10g of alcohol. A first step to supporting a client to understand their alcohol consumption, is to encourage them to quantify their drinking in standard drinks, rather than by the glass/stubby/can. There are so many mixes and strengths of alcohol, therefore by referring to standard drinks we have an accurate account of the amount of alcohol being consumed. Current national guidelines describe low risk drinking as no more than 10 standard drinks in a seven-day period, consuming no more than four standard drinks on any one day. Further recommendations are that young people under the age of 18 should not drink at all, and for women trying to fall pregnant, pregnant women and breastfeeding mothers, the safest option is to abstain[2].

For all other drugs, many clinicians are concerned that they won't understand the language the client uses and are oblivious to how particular drugs are measured. Remember, you don't need to be an expert! Ask your client to explain the terminology they use, and how their drug is measured. Slang terms are common and can leave clinicians completely confused. Take consolation in knowing that even those clinicians who specialise in substance use, regularly ask clients to explain their jargon! The jargon can change depending on locality, and the client's age or culture. In my experience clients love teaching me and take delight in the fact that I am willing to learn from them.

Consider referral

Once you've determined what, how much and when the client is using, consider (with the client's consent) phoning your local alcohol and other drugs service for advice. They can inform if an extensive assessment is required or reassure that it is safe for you to continue working with your client without additional specialist services. Local AOD services can also advise you of additional supports that are available in your community, such as peer support groups. Additionally, there are a growing number of online and app-based tools that can be a great compliment to the support you are providing.

Application

I have been in the situation many times where the client has already stopped drinking and is in active withdrawal on the day of consultation. This adds to the complexity of the situation and must be managed accordingly. In these circumstances, the person needs immediate medical assessment to manage risk and ensure their physical safety.

I can hear all my readers squirming; how is it possible to arrange immediate medical assessment? Doctors aren't on speed dial! I hear you! More often than not, such clients don't have any money left to pay for a doctor, medication or alcohol, they have no support systems in place, and they live alone (or are homeless).

In these cases, there's no other option except for them to present to the emergency department or call an ambulance. Safety is the ultimate priority in these cases. For any other drug,

All or Nothing

apart from alcohol or benzodiazepines, immediate medical attention is not always necessary. Withdrawal will be extremely uncomfortable and unpleasant, but there's not necessarily a requirement for the client to be medically supervised. In all cases of active withdrawal, it is safest to consult with your local AOD specialty service for advice.

What if your client has set themselves an abstinence goal, but constantly lapses and is struggling with feelings of failure? Firstly, consider if the client's environment is conducive to abstinence, or are they surrounded by too many temptations and triggers? Perhaps, if abstinence is their priority, considering a residential rehabilitation setting might be appropriate, where they can be supported in a therapeutic environment.

What about those clients who recognise that abstinence is not the right goal for them, however their family are demanding it? Ultimatums are declared; if the client uses again the family will cut them off. I've seen this many times when working with families who have reached their limit. Education and support for the family is imperative, assisting them to gain a better understanding of the cycle of addiction, and how to access agencies that can support their needs as caregivers. Wherever possible, giving the family a break by the client temporarily moving out to other accommodation or residential rehabilitation can ease tensions, and provide space for treatment plans to be established.

Ultimatums do put a lot of pressure on the client and can themselves be triggers for lapses. This is particularly difficult for the client who has been using their substance to cope with stress. With support, rather than extreme ultimatums, families can discuss and decide upon boundaries and consequences.

ACTION POINTS

- Include a substance use diary in your AOD toolbox (consider apps also).

- Have information readily available for your clients regarding risks of sudden abstinence, particularly for alcohol and benzodiazepines. Prepare a list of GPs in your area who are taking new clients, and those who bulk bill.

- Provide details of SMART Recovery (harm reduction-based peer support group) as well as AA/NA (abstinence-based peer support group) to your clients so that they can make an informed choice.

CHAPTER 6

Detox

Great things are not done by impulse, but by a series of small things brought together.

Vincent Van Gogh

Many clients and their families don't understand what detox is and its purpose. Additionally, clinicians and service providers frequently misunderstand the definition and role of detox in recovery. The term detox is often used as if it's the cure or the solution to addiction. There are numerous ways to detox and in fact, detox isn't necessary for every recovery plan.

Understanding when detox is essential in recovery will ensure it is chosen appropriately. For clients choosing moderation over abstinence, detox isn't always necessary, because withdrawal symptoms can be avoided by slow reduction of the substance. Detox can be achieved by various methods, and in a variety of settings. It's a common misconception that hospitalisation is required for detox – conversely, many detoxes can be completed safely in the home environment. There is not a one size fits all solution. Therefore, it is imperative that long-term goals are explored with the client to ascertain if a detox is required, and if so, what environment is right for them.

It's also important to understand that detox may or may not need medication to assist. Many people detox regularly from their drug of choice and they do it without any form of medication to assist them. It's so important as clinicians to understand that detox is only a very small part of the recovery process; that spending a week or two away from the substance is not, in most cases, going to be enough to support ongoing abstinence or moderation. In most cases, it's just a very small start of a lifetime journey of recovery.

Most people don't know that if alcohol dependent drinkers frequently detox, only to relapse on each occasion, that their brain becomes more sensitive to changes in the neurotransmitters. Repeating this cycle of detox and relapse puts the person at a higher risk of withdrawal complications such as seizures and delirium tremens, which are life threatening. This condition of increased neurotransmitter sensitivity is known as kindling[1]. Such withdrawal complications make it vitally important to partner an intention to detox with a comprehensive support plan for long-term recovery. In this chapter we're going to define detox, how detox is achieved and how it fits into the recovery journey.

Detox

What is detox?

Detox is an abbreviation for detoxification, the process of clearing toxins from the body. In substance use, detox is generally referring to the body metabolising the drug and clearing the drug from the body's systems. When undergoing detox, it is at this time that the person will experience physical symptoms of withdrawal, as detox requires abstinence. Depending on the drug, it generally lasts between a few days and a few weeks to complete a detox and clear the toxic effects of the drug from the body. Some people experience very mild symptoms, where for others the experience of withdrawal is traumatic.

Severity of withdrawal is dependent on:

- length of time using the drug
- classification of the drug
- age and physical health
- emotional state
- method of withdrawal[2].

Although symptoms of physical withdrawal can subside within days, emotional and psychological symptoms such as cravings, irritability and mood swings can take much longer to resolve. This is one of the reasons physical detox or withdrawal alone usually doesn't sustain ongoing abstinence. The aim of detox is not to be a standalone treatment, but to prepare the client to participate in ongoing rehabilitation[3].

Before you start up a ladder, count the rungs.
                                    Yiddish proverb.

How to detox

Hospital detox

Hospital admissions may be recommended for detox if the person is at risk of complicated withdrawal because of a history of seizures or delirium. Persons who are frail or have medical or psychiatric comorbidities are also at risk of withdrawal complications and close medical supervision is recommended[4]. Pharmacological intervention is often required for withdrawal from alcohol, sedatives and opioid class drugs to manage the symptoms and keep the client safe, as withdrawal from these types of substances can be life threatening[5]. Often hospital admissions for detox are unplanned, as the client presents to the emergency department requiring immediate medical treatment. Once the medical emergency has passed the patient is discharged, and if not followed up with comprehensive support with relevant services, long-term recovery outcomes are unfavourable. Some hospitals have an AOD Consultation Liaison position whose role is to engage with these inpatients and facilitate linkage and referral to support services upon discharge[6].

Community residential detox

Frequently clients and their families want admission to a facility to complete a detox. I can't speak for all locations, but in regional Queensland, Australia, there are very few facilities providing residential detox. Generally, programs in residential withdrawal units last up to 10 days, and medication is sometimes prescribed to provide symptomatic treatment.

Detox

In localities without a residential withdrawal unit, the person may need to travel if they wish to access this service. Because of the rarity of such residential detox facilities, waiting times can be lengthy, creating additional barriers to access. Some residential rehabs also provide residential detox to complement their program, which is supportive of continuity of care.

Home-based withdrawal

For clients with mild to moderate dependence, home-based withdrawal may be considered. This is only recommended if the client is withdrawing from a single substance and has no history of complex withdrawal, and no significant physical or mental health comorbidities. To safely detox at home, the client must also have access to a support person who can stay with them. The client and their family can be supported by their GP, and an outpatient AOD clinic. Medications prescribed are often dispensed from a community pharmacy or AOD service daily, and withdrawal symptoms monitored. Many people successfully withdraw from drugs or alcohol at home, and many prefer this as it is less disruptive to their lives. It is my experience that relapse is less common after a home detox in comparison to a hospital detox, as the client has ceased their substance in familiar surroundings, overcoming common triggers from day one of the detox. When a client withdraws in hospital, relapse can be triggered upon returning to their familiar home environment associated with their drug taking.

Keep Calm and Treat Addiction

Detox in perspective

Before admission to many residential rehabilitation services, it will be expected that the client has cleared their body system of substances of dependence. For some clients, this will require a medically supervised detox either at home or in a facility or hospital. Planning is of vital importance in these circumstances. Once a client has an admission date for a residential rehab, a specialist AOD service can work with the client to ensure they complete a detox in the week leading up to their admission, making sure there's no gap between their detox and their admission to rehab. In most of these circumstances, multiple services are required to coordinate care, with the client being central to the process. It is best for the client to ensure they are aware of the detox policy of their chosen rehab, to make certain they are well prepared for admission.

> *Quitting smoking is easy, I've done it thousands of times.*
> Mark Twain

Often underestimated is the detox after the detox! Although the body can physically be cleansed from the drug within weeks, the brain is another matter. There are significant impacts on the neurotransmitters of the brain when a person has been using substances for a lengthy period. This time of adjustment is also known as post-acute withdrawal and is the stage where the neurotransmitters of the brain repair and adjust to life without the chemical additives. During this time, it is common for the person to experience irritability, mood swings, depression, and problems with sleep, memory and attention. These symptoms can come and go in waves and can last many months after physically withdrawing[7].

Detox

For clients experiencing this, it can feel like all their efforts are in vain; what's the point of doing this if I am going to feel this bad forever? It is important to emphasise that this condition is temporary and will in time resolve. For clients conditioned to receiving immediate rewards from drug taking, sitting with this discomfort can be extremely difficult. This once again highlights the need for ongoing support in the weeks and sometimes months following detox.

Application

Many clients or their families demand inpatient detox. I can't count the number of times that families have been hostile because I can't organise for their loved one to be hospitalised immediately for detox. Furthermore, other service providers have equally resented my inability to conjure up a hospital bed. In these cases, the only solution is to calmly explain to the client and their family that there are limited resources, and admission to hospital is often out of our sphere of influence or control. Reiterate that detoxes are best prearranged, and part of a wider recovery plan to ensure best outcomes and provide them with a list of state-wide residential detox facilities to contact. If your client or their loved ones continue their demands for urgency, refer them to their GP or hospital emergency department for medical advice.

What happens if the client is in active withdrawal already? In these circumstances, the person needs immediate medical assessment to manage risk and ensure their physical safety, either with the GP, AOD specialist service or hospital emergency department. This is unfortunately a familiar occurrence in my practice, and forces reactive treatment rather than proactive recovery. There are diverse reasons for this presentation, the most common including financial difficulty, deterioration in physical health, pressure from family and a sense of hopelessness. Once the client has been medically stabilised, it is beneficial to explore the risks of these presentations to encourage the client to adopt alternative, safer approaches to help-seeking in the future.

For those clients who have tried numerous times at home to detox and find that they just can't stick it out to complete withdrawal, it may be time to consider alternatives. Firstly, is a detox necessary? Perhaps slow reduction may be an option before cutting out the substance entirely. Sometimes reducing the drug can facilitate progression to detox. It may be wise to consider a residential detox, so that the client has a protective environment to support their efforts to quit. Most importantly, appreciating the efforts and energy the client is dedicating to their recovery acknowledges their progress in a strengths-based framework.

Detox

ACTION POINTS

- Talk to your local drug and alcohol service to understand the local options available for detox, and be familiar with referral processes.

- Have resources in your AOD toolbox explaining acute withdrawal for various substances and what to expect.

- Network and find out which local GPs have a special interest in addiction treatment and keep a list of these for your clients at risk of withdrawal.

CHAPTER 7

Rehab

Rehab is one thing, but it takes years to get that attitude adjustment.

Johnny Colt

Once acute withdrawal or detox is completed, the client enters the next phase of their recovery journey. A comprehensive support plan following detox can comprise of accessing outpatient services, or admission to a rehab. Rehab is an abbreviation for a drug and alcohol residential rehabilitation program. It is a common misconception that rehab is required for successful recovery from substance addiction. Rehab is sometimes required but is not the appropriate choice in every situation. Recovery can occur in a normal everyday environment whilst accessing outpatient AOD services. In fact, like detoxes completed at home, the person develops resilience early in their recovery, having to deal with and overcome their triggers and cravings in an uncontrolled, familiar environment.

Like detox facilities, rehabs can be difficult to access – they are a limited resource. It is likely that the client will need to travel outside of their town of residence to access a rehab facility. Additionally, most rehabs have waiting lists, and clients can endure lengthy waits for admission. It is important to consider if a rehab is the appropriate choice for your client, particularly young people with lower levels of dependence. Remember a rehab is a facility where that young person is going to reside with many others who may have been dependent on substances for a lot longer than them. I have had family members of a teenager occasionally smoking cannabis, wanting to pack them off to a rehab. Potentially a rehab environment will introduce this young person to information they might not have otherwise learnt, such as intravenous use of drugs, so caution is advised. Residential rehab is best considered for clients exhibiting high dependence.

For those clients who are working or who have financial commitments such as mortgages, rehab is not always viable. Clients in stable employment may be unable to access leave to attend rehab, and potential loss of their job could be detrimental to their long-term recovery. These are important considerations because, like detox, rehab is only a small part of the recovery process. Rehab is not a cure; evidence shows that the risk of relapse after residential rehab is high[1]. Rather, it is provision of an environment to completely focus on recovery. There are less distractions of everyday life, enabling the person

Rehab

to dedicate time to addressing their addiction. The clients I work with who benefit from rehab, are the ones who commit wholeheartedly to the process. Just existing at rehab is not going to support sustained change on discharge. Rehab is simply a tool for recovery, and those who productively utilise their time in rehab, and engage in support following discharge, reap the rewards moving forward.

Clinicians can automatically recommend rehab without fully understanding its function and relevance to recovery. Advising rehab can deter some clients from treatment because they are just not prepared to live in a facility, with a bunch of strangers, for a lengthy period. Wrongly presenting rehab as the answer supports unrealistic expectations that rehab is the ultimate solution. False beliefs are adopted by the client, regarding rehab as their genie in a bottle.

I've worked with lots of clients over the years both pre and post rehab. Unfortunately, it is common to complete rehab, only to return to substance use within days or weeks of discharge. Think about a time where you have gone on a strict diet. Imagine being on that strict diet for three months, losing a whole heap of weight and feeling on top of the world. To be successful, gym membership was required, along with a dietician and weight-loss support groups. Then imagine after losing weight, quitting the gym, not going to the dietician and giving up support group attendance. It is likely all that weight is going to creep back on, and then some! Similarly, if a person leaves rehab and returns to the behaviours and environments that were previously central to their lives when they were using substances, chances are they will relapse. The skills learnt in rehab need to be applied to life outside of the security of rehab, for the client to be able to move forward in the recovery process. Likewise, planning is required while still in rehab to ensure the client has supports and resources in place ready for discharge, such as counsellors, peer support groups and supportive accommodation. In this chapter we're going to explore what rehab is, the indications for rehab, how to access it and where rehab fits in the recovery journey.

What is rehab?

Residential rehabs require a high level of commitment from clients, as they involve living in a residential centre for a period of time, usually ranging between 12 weeks and 12 months. Rehabs are completely voluntary; the client is free to walk out at any time!!! It is a common misconception that the client is contained in the rehab, and even held against their will. Rehab can be beneficial particularly for people who don't have a stable home situation or need a break from their current environment. Rehabs are abstinence based, meaning there isn't any allowance for drug or alcohol use. It is important to clarify with the rehab which drugs are excluded; some exclude nicotine and prescribed drugs of dependence. Each rehab is different, and it is important for clients to contact the rehab and discuss the specific programs offered, to consider if they are the right fit for them.

Rehabs can be:

- gender specific
- religious or faith based. For those clients who already have positive affiliations with a religious

Rehab

  background, this can be a suitable and supportive option
- age specific, e.g. rehab programs specifically for younger people
- for indigenous clients exclusively
- attached to a detox program.

Residential rehabs normally offer structured programs inclusive of any number of the following:

- therapy/counselling, both individual and group
- development of life skills including meal planning and preparation
- physical exercise
- mindfulness and meditation
- education and information, inclusive of practical strategies
- support to access providers such as GPs, psychologists, job networks, housing.

It's important for your client to investigate what therapies are offered by the rehab, and the costs involved, as this varies between facilities. Many take a percentage of the client's government benefit to cover costs of the accommodation and program, whilst some are costly and covered by private health insurance. It's important that the client does the research, rings up the rehab and discovers all the nuances of each, to discover which one is right for them[2].

Programs usually involve both individual and group peer-based therapy. Relapse prevention is a large component of the program, exploring how to maintain abstinence post-discharge from the facility. Clients often have access to exercise programs, are responsible for some grocery shopping, preparation of meals and household chores and are supported to access health care such as GPs and dentists.

Access explained

Rehabs generally have quite a lengthy waitlist, and it can take some time from when the client decides they want to go to rehab, to when they are actually admitted. The moment a client decides they are interested in rehab, it is imperative that they contact several facilities, to get their name added to the waitlists as soon as possible. Without being on the waitlist, there is never going to be an option to access rehab. Most commonly, the rehabs do not want to talk to the clinician or the family, they want to talk to the client. This is understandable considering that rehab is completely voluntary; they need to know that the client has made the decision to apply of their own accord. In my experience, getting the client to make the call and get their name added to the waitlist can be a challenge.

Although rehabs may indicate that there is a three-month wait, admission to rehab can sometimes be realised in a shorter timeframe. Should existing clients exit the rehab prematurely, the rehab generally starts calling people on the waitlist to fill the vacant position. Although rehabs may have 30 people on the waitlist, commonly it is difficult to reach people, or their situation may have changed since applying and they no longer want admission. If your client is motivated to access rehab, they are best advised to phone the facility coordinator weekly, to advise of their continued interest for admission, ensuring their contact details are up to date.

Rehab in perspective

When considering rehab, the client is encouraged to contemplate whether rehab matches their long-term goals. Rehab is supportive of abstinence, mostly operating within an abstinence model rather than a harm minimisation model. However, even if a client intends to attempt moderation after discharge, rehab can still be a beneficial time to reset, learn life skills and practical strategies.

An alternative to residential rehab is a day rehab program. This is an accessible option for those clients for whom residing in a facility is not feasible. Commonly known as day-habs, these programs are generally run on weekdays over four to six weeks, enabling clients to return to their own home at the end of the day. This option is less intense, providing more flexibility. For those clients with severe dependence, this freedom can result in relapse as they remain surrounded by familiar triggers and risky situations at home[3].

Like residential rehabs, day-habs most commonly have limited availability and waiting lists. For both residential and day programs, there may be a requirement for the client to complete a detox prior to entering the program. It is important to consider what the treatment plan is post-discharge from rehab programs. Some rehab programs offer after-care plans for support in assimilating with normal life.

Keep Calm and Treat Addiction

One of the things that's often forgotten about drug rehabilitation, it's not a destiny. It's a journey.

Peter Hobson

Application

It can be challenging, and at times distressing for the clinician when the family or the client comes in demanding an immediate admission to rehab. This comes from a misconception that rehabs are plentiful, and easily accessed, and are an essential requirement for recovery. In these cases, it is important to keep calm and not get caught up in the panic. As a clinician, provide education to the client and their family. They can be provided with a list of rehabs to contact and research for themselves. Most people aren't aware that the client themselves is required to contact the rehab directly, and that it can't be organised by a third party.

What if your client is perfectly suited to rehab and really motivated for admission, but there are no places available and potentially months to wait? Honestly, I find myself in this situation regularly, and it can be devastating for all concerned. For those clients with severe dependence who are unable to address their addiction outside of a residential rehab, this is especially difficult. Layering of support is essential in these situations; think about what other services can be involved in supporting your client. One service isn't enough, a wrap-around approach is required.

Consider thinking outside of the box: are there other solutions for provision of a safe environment? Eighteen-year-old Jimmy

Rehab

with a severe methamphetamine dependence was able to go and stay with his cousins who lived out of town, well away from the temptations that triggered him daily. Although not ideal, if this is a safe option for your client it can result in successful outcomes. Jimmy was without a car or licence and unable to impulsively access his drug-using friends. Whilst at his cousin's farm, he was able to support them with physical labor which provided a welcome distraction. Jimmy was able to access counselling support online, inclusive of SMART Recovery peer support groups. His family brought him into town once a week to access counselling. When a rehab vacancy became available, Jimmy decided he no longer required it, furthermore, his self-esteem was enhanced knowing all that he had achieved with the support of his family.

Thirty-five-year-old Matthew is an example of a particularly challenging recovery journey. Matthew had successfully completed rehab three times over the preceding five years, only to relapse soon after each discharge. In fact, most recently Matthew had discharged himself from rehab soon after admission, to arrive at the AOD service help-seeking, intoxicated, and requesting another admission to rehab. In situations like these, it's important to remember the lifelong nature of addiction recovery. Rehabs can be difficult environments for clients to tolerate; there are many personalities, some possibly with anti-social traits, living together in a confined environment. This clearly would be challenging at any time, more so for clients working through their own issues and coping with withdrawal. Every time a client walks in the door, there is an opportunity to reflect on what has gone before them to create a stronger plan. Despite rehab not being effective in the past, the next admission could be life changing.

Keep Calm and Treat Addiction

ACTION POINTS

- Compile a list of rehab options to provide to your clients seeking rehab, inclusive of contact details so that they can complete their own research.

- Consult with your local AOD service and understand the options available, and the necessary referral processes.

- Be ready to sit with your client and support them when they are ready to contact rehabs – it can be daunting alone. Most rehabs will take a name and number and call back later. Support your client in following up enquiries regularly.

CHAPTER 8

Rock Bottom

He waited for the black, terrible anger as though for some beast out of the night. But it did not come to him. His bowels seemed weighted with lead, and he walked slowly and lingered against fences and the cold, wet walls of buildings by the way. Descent into the depths until at last there was no further chasm below. He touched the solid bottom of despair and there took ease.

Carson McCullers

It's often said that a person won't change until they have hit rock bottom, and at this point they'll finally give in and accept treatment for their drug issue. Families or friends will often bring their loved one into counselling when they believe the person has finally reached rock bottom and they are ready for change. Some family and friends will disown the person in the hope this accelerates their arrival at rock bottom, so that then they're motivated to change. Rock bottom is a dangerous myth and not a concept that is helpful for either the person using substances or their family and friends.

So why is rock bottom a risky concept? Firstly, rock bottom has a different definition for each person. What I might consider would be someone's rock bottom, isn't necessarily considered by them as rock bottom, nor is it always a motivation for them to change. Assuming that the substance user is going to see their situation with the same lens as the family or clinician is not conducive to a therapeutic alliance.

Secondly, it's precarious to assume that because we consider the client as being at rock bottom, treatment is going to somehow be easier for them to commit to. Treatment still looks as scary and overwhelming at rock bottom as anywhere else on the continuum. Just because someone is at a low point in life, doesn't mean they're necessarily going to engage in treatment.

Furthermore, there's often a lot of pressure on the drug user when others consider them to be at rock bottom. Family can be driven by fear; if someone doesn't intervene right now at this crisis point, the opportunity for treatment might be missed. This simply isn't true because people change at all points in the continuum, not just when we believe they've reached their lowest. It's important to keep the lines of communication open, no matter where the person is in their journey with addiction. Forcing someone into treatment creates resentment, and the likelihood that the substance user will distance themselves from the very people they need.

Tony Trimingham, founder of Family Drug Support and a father who has suffered the tragic loss of his son to heroin, refers to the 'masculine' and 'feminine' responses to a loved one's addiction[1]. He concludes neither is helpful; the masculine reaction attempting to control the drug user by threats and ultimatums, whilst the feminine response aims to be protective and keep peace in the household by disguising the drug user's behaviour that will upset others in the family. While it's vital for loved ones to not give up on them, enabling the behaviour of the substance user is not helpful. Boundaries are required, along with unconditional love – but not approval.

The tragedy is that rock bottom represents death for some substance users. Desiring or compelling someone to reach rock bottom, that mythical place where change is to be realised, catastrophically can result in death. Waiting or forcing rock bottom may seem like a solution, when in reality it results in the person feeling isolated and hopeless and more vulnerable to harm.

So how do families, friends and loved ones provide support to someone who is continuing in self-damaging behaviour, without cutting them off or having their own life become as chaotic as the drug user? As a clinician working in the field of addiction, sitting alongside families in this situation is one of my most difficult responsibilities. Witnessing their devastation, distress and helplessness; hearing them blame themselves and each other, is disturbing. This chapter will unpack three principles families can explore with the clinician to ensure everyone in the family, inclusive of the person using drugs, is cared for and protected.

Keep Calm and Treat Addiction

Boundaries

Supportive parents and loved ones are the most powerful encouragers of recovery[2]. However, provision of this support can take its toll on families. Establishing realistic boundaries in addition to reasonable consequences is an important ingredient for family survival. Likewise, allowing natural consequences to behaviour supports recovery. I am all-too familiar with parents frantically arranging drug and alcohol counselling for their adult child who has a court date looming, in an effort to lessen the penalty incurred. Need I say, as tempting as this is for the parents, it is not helpful.

Most parents are familiar with the concept of boundaries, and boundaries in drug use are no different. Healthy boundaries promote mental and emotional stability for all concerned[3]. Consistency is important, saying what you mean and meaning what you say. Sitting down and talking with your loved one, agreeing on consequences for behaviour, and then reliably observing these are important elements of boundary implementation. Additionally, having a drug problem doesn't exclude the client from discussing boundaries for the rest of the family. Using drugs does not take away all rights to having a say in the family. Boundaries work both ways, and the discussion should include boundaries and consequences for the rest of the family around behaviours that the client finds unhelpful in their recovery.

When families are setting boundaries, it is imperative for them to be prepared for the imminent breaking of boundaries, requiring a timely, firm response according to the agreed consequences[4]. This is difficult for families, and it is recommended they are engaged in counselling of their own or involved in a relevant peer support group. Families often fall into the trap of becoming a doormat in their quest to be supportive. Family members and support persons are not required to put up with anything and everything at all costs. It is crucial all family members discuss and agree on boundaries and consequences. Furthermore, when it comes time for implementing consequences of boundary breaches, a united approach is essential.

Behaviour

When acknowledging a boundary has been broken and implementing consequences, the following are vital for the family to consider:

- calm down first; don't react in anger
- make a suitable time to have a discussion; it may be appropriate to wait
- be sure to react to the behaviour, not the person[4].

Once families resort to name calling and shaming, nobody wins. As hard as it is, communication is best kept as ordered and composed as possible.

Families are to be encouraged to remember the substance user beyond their substance use. Complimenting them on things that they are doing well and focusing on other positive aspects of their character is valuable[5]. It is easy to be all-consumed with the drug use of the individual, forgetting all else about them. However, praise needs to be authentic, and not fabricated if it simply isn't true.

Keep Calm and Treat Addiction

Safety is of top priority, of both the substance user and family members. Violence should never be tolerated. Unfortunately, it is common to see situations where family members are living in fear, tolerating abusive, aggressive behaviour, terrified if they refuse to endure the behaviour, their loved one will harm themselves. Safety plans can be developed with the family, to ensure that there are strategies in place to respond to risky situations. Families are to be urged not to confront the person when they are: hanging out for drugs, under the influence of drugs, or coming down from drugs[6].

Key elements of a safety plan include:

- a list of phone numbers to access help quickly, e.g. police, mental health emergency team, neighbour
- ascertain a place where a private phone call can be made
- pinpoint a safe place where family members can go if required, e.g. friend's house
- have the things needed easily accessible if a quick getaway is required e.g. important documents, identification, bank details, phone[7].

Police may need to be involved; domestic violence orders may be required. Nevertheless, this does not equate to an unsupportive family. Relationships can continue within the limits and boundaries of these rules and regulations. These are simply a consequence for behaviour, and don't define severed relationships. These consequences can be discussed in boundary conversations, should aggression be an issue.

Rock Bottom

Self-care

It's important for families and friends to remember that the recovery journey is likely to be lengthy, making it vital that self-care is considered. Often families forsake themselves, to focus on the family member with the drug issue. It seems that everyone else is forgotten in an overwhelming urge to 'fix' the situation and get things back to normal. It is common for families and friends to withdraw from their support networks and become isolated[8]. Sometimes the shame and stigma associated with substance use further segregates the family in the plight to keep it all secretive.

Tony Trimingham compares families dealing with a loved one's drug use to walking a tightrope; being pushed out of the familiar, to a place that is frightening and foreign.

He describes the natural human response in this circumstance is to seek a safety net, which is often one of the following:

- throw the person out of home (or end the relationship) to make them hit 'rock bottom' so they will change
- get the person into treatment to fix them
- get the formula, the wonder drug, or the magical cure which will be the solution.

He explains that these things don't work, and the family finds themselves back walking the tightrope, often two steps behind their previous position, more frightened than ever.

It is identified that tightrope walkers carry a pole, to keep their balance, to make the walk easier. Tony likens the balance pole to the activities and resources the family members usually access to lead a balanced life, yet these are the things most people let go of when faced with the crisis of a loved one using substances. He stresses the importance of the family and loved ones supporting the substance user to hold on to their balance pole, or if they have dropped it, to pick it back up again. Looking after physical, mental and emotional health ensures the family has the resilience and strength for the recovery journey ahead[9].

> *I believe my son would've got to that point (of change)... eventually... I don't know when. You never know when. That's why we believe in harm minimisation because we believe in keeping people safe and well until they can make those decisions.*
>
> Tony Trimingham

Application

Very few things trouble me more than seeing ageing parents struggling with an adult child with a drug or alcohol problem. One such example is Martha (73), with her 44-year-old son, Eric who has battled an alcohol dependency his entire life. Martha looks at me with tired, sad eyes, expressing her fear that if she doesn't continue to meet Eric's demands, he will kill himself. Here is an example of a gentle conversation regarding boundaries and consequences.

Martha: I just can't do it anymore. Eric can't stay at home if he keeps drinking. I'm getting too old.

Rock Bottom

Eric: I promise I won't drink again Mum. You can't kick me out.

Tania: Eric, if you can't live at home, what would be your options?

Eric: I would have to live on the streets and would probably end up dead.

Tania: What other options are there Eric? When you haven't been able to live at home before, where did you go?

Eric: Well I did have that unit, and I have been at the men's hostel. But I hate it there, I want to be at home.

Tania: It sounds like you would prefer to be at home, and there are other options you could access if you needed somewhere to stay.

Eric: I just want to go home.

Tania: You want to live at home, and your mum is feeling worn out. Martha, you and Eric have identified that a residential rehab is the next step in his recovery?

Martha: Yes, but Eric says he wants to go, but when a bed comes up, he won't go. Nothing else has helped, I want him to go to rehab.

Eric: I'll go Mum, if you'll just let me come home.

Tania: That's great Eric. How about you phone the rehab now to put your name down on the waiting list. *Eric phones the rehab.*

Tania: Now where to from here Martha?

Martha: Well he can stay until he gets a rehab bed, but if he won't go… I can't do this anymore.

Tania: Eric, your mum really cares about you, and is willing for you to stay with her if you accept a rehab bed when it becomes available. It is your decision whether to go to rehab. Should you choose not to accept the bed, she has said that she can't have you at home. What would be your options should this happen?

Keep Calm and Treat Addiction

Eric: I guess I'd have to go to the shelter, but I won't, I'll go to rehab.

Tania: So, it's agreed that Eric will stay with you Martha, until he can be admitted to rehab. If Eric chooses not to go to rehab when a bed is available, he will move out of home into alternative accommodation. In the meantime, let's talk about supports we can put in place for Eric to access while waiting for the admission, and some support for you too Martha.

When it comes time to go to rehab, unfortunately Eric refuses to accept the admission. I would like to say that Martha held fast to the plan, and Eric went to the men's shelter. But this isn't a fairytale, and I'm not a miracle worker.

Rock Bottom

ACTION POINTS

- Compile a list of support options for the family/carers inclusive of counselling and peer support groups (both face to face and online).

- Ensure the family know who to call in times of emergency, e.g. police, ambulance, mental health.

- Encourage the family/carers to access education for themselves, through courses (face to face and online) or reading.

PART C

JOURNEY

Change is a process, not an event.

James Prochaska

Stages of Change

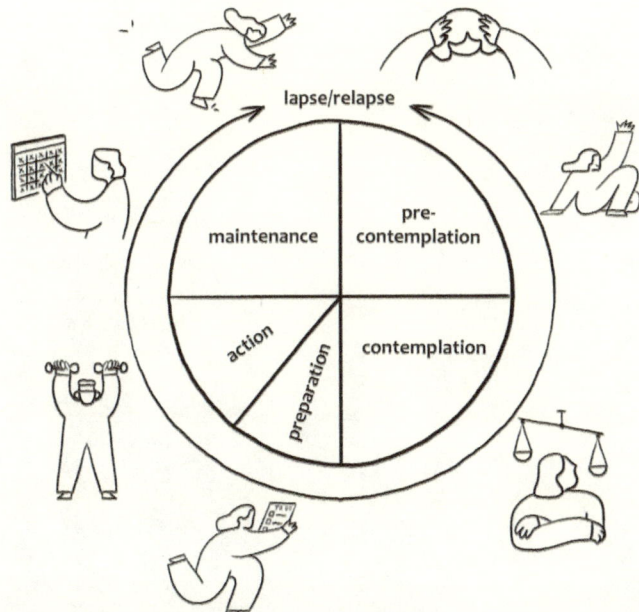

CHAPTER 9

Permission

There's no key to great relationships, there's simply a well-worn welcome mat.

Curtis Tyrone Jones

The precontemplative stage is a difficult stage for friends and family of the person using substances, likewise it can be challenging for the clinician. In this stage, the person is not inclined to change what they are doing. In fact, they're happy with their current lifestyle, and satisfied with life. It's important to give the person permission to choose their path forward. Of equal importance is to keep the person as safe as possible, as well as the people around them, and the community, while they are in this stage.

Keep Calm and Treat Addiction

At precontemplation, the client is likely to be defensive, and suspicious of the trustworthiness and motives of the clinician[1]. Treating the client as if they are ready for change will be likely to end in disengagement, as the person does not recognise there is a problem to solve. Believing that the clinician is judging them and pressuring them for change is not conducive to a therapeutic relationship. Any parent who has nagged their teenager to clean their room will relate to the reality that if the teenager is not concerned about their untidy room, no amount of pestering is going to make it happen! In fact, the more the parent talks about it, the less likely it becomes.

When in precontemplation, it is important to focus on strategies to minimise the impacts of the substance on the client's physical and mental health, keeping them as safe as possible. This concept is called harm reduction, and is widely misunderstood by the general public, furthermore by many health professionals. Harm reduction is a harm minimisation approach, this being defined by the Australian Government Department of Health as addressing:

> *alcohol and other drug issues by reducing the harmful effects of alcohol and other drugs on individuals and society.*[2]

Harm minimisation doesn't condone or increase drug use as many wrongly believe; harm minimisation acknowledges that people will choose to use substances regardless of the risks and recognises the importance of preventing and reducing drug-related problems for both the person and their community.

Accepting that the client uses drugs or alcohol does not equate to agreeing with their choices. Rather, this approach focuses on reduction of negative impacts on the client's:

Permission

- physical health
- mental health
- relationships
- criminality
- employment and finances.

By focusing on the reduction of harm for the client rather than attempting to enforce the elimination or reduction of the drug use, harms and risks are reduced for the wider community. Additionally, harm minimisation saves money and resources for our health system and government. Harm reduction strategies are much more cost effective than punitive measures such as policing and imprisonment[3]. While the clinician is focusing on harm reduction rather than drug elimination, therapeutic alliance and trust is built with the client, a crucial foundation for future recovery.

The following are examples of harm reduction strategies:

Strategy	Description	Rationale
Needle and syringe programs	Anonymous service provision of free sterile injecting equipment and disposal units	- Reduction of bloodborne viruses such as hepatitis B and C and HIV - Reduction of injection-related injuries such as abscesses - Reduction of incorrect disposal of used needles and syringes hence reducing public risk[4]

Keep Calm and Treat Addiction

Strategy	Description	Rationale
Medication assisted opioid treatment programs	Combination of medication and supportive counselling. Medications can include methadone or buprenorphine, and benefits can include elimination of withdrawal, reduced cravings and blocking of other opioids if used.	• Prevention of death through fatal overdose • Reduction of bloodborne viruses • Reduced impact on relationships, finances/employment, crime • Cost savings to health, legal systems and social services[5]
Pill testing	Provision of pill testing to people considering using a substance to identify what they are taking. A range of information (inclusive of risks) is provided to assist the person to make an informed decision.	• Reduction of drugs consumed • Reduction of variety of drugs consumed in an episode, thereby reducing risk[6]

Permission

Strategy	Description	Rationale
Medically supervised injecting rooms	Allow for a safer environment for people who inject drugs, where health education and access to services can also be provided.	• Reduced deaths from overdose and harms from rushed injecting • Reduction of bloodborne viruses • Reduction of drug-related crime • Reduction of incorrect disposal of used needles and syringes[7]

Across the world, 17.8% of people who inject drugs are living with HIV – however, in Australia, due to our good harm reduction strategies, only 1.1% of people who inject drugs are living with HIV. This is incredibly low compared to the global figure of 17.8%, Eastern Europe's figure of 24.7%, and North America's figure of 9%. These countries have much less effective harm reduction strategies than Australia does, resulting in much higher rates of HIV infection in their populations[8].

In Australia's economic history, for every $1 spent on needle and syringe programs, our country saves $27. That's $27 saved for every dollar spent![3] If we choose to turn our back on harm minimisation, this increases the burden of disease, and the number of people carrying bloodborne viruses. Ignoring harm minimisation potentially increases the number of used needles in parks and gardens rather than being correctly disposed of. Ultimately, failing to adequately implement harm minimisation strategies, can not only result in harm for the person using the drug, but also the extended community.

In this chapter, we will explore how to identify a client in precontemplation, and the best interventions for the clinician to utilise at this time.

> *I see harm reduction as a way of engaging people as part of that path to recovery.*
>
> Paul R Ehrlich

The happy user

The precontemplater is often referred to as the 'happy user'. There is no intention to change; no recognition for the need to change. Many young people experimenting with substances are in this stage. Clients who have been coerced by family members to attend and clients advised by their solicitors to attend to 'look good' for court often present as happy users. Introducing a formal assessment process too early, can interfere with development of therapeutic alliance, the essential foundation for recovery. As tempting as it is to complete an assessment on the first visit, the best approach is to focus on engagement and rapport building[9].

Here are some comments I commonly hear from clients in precontemplation:

- It's natural, it's from a bush, it should be legal
- Some people have a drink, I have a cone, there's nothing wrong with it

Permission

- I'm not hurting anyone; I wish people would mind their own business.

Sometimes evidence of precontemplation can be absolute denial. I have seen many court-directed clients tell me they were 'in the wrong place at the wrong time', or they took the blame for a mate, or had it planted on them, or their food laced. Now these claims could be true, or the client could be in precontemplation, avoiding having to talk about it. Either way, the approach is the same; don't judge, believe what they say and work with it. This might be your one chance to engage and demonstrate to the client that when they are ready to change, you are the right person to talk to. Clients in precontemplation can be hostile; move your conversation to common ground, something both you and the client can agree on. Be curious and explore what matters to them.

Information sharing

There may be an opportunity to share information with the client if they allow. Asking permission prior to communicating this is a good approach. If your client is injecting, as part of your therapeutic discussion, ask them if they are aware of the needle and syringe programs nearest to them, and the importance of not sharing needles and equipment. If this is raised with a spirit of concern for the client, it is mostly well received.

Assisting the client to care for their physical health is important at the precontemplation stage. Does your client have a regular GP, and when is the last time they had a checkup? People who use substances often neglect their physical health as their substance use increases. Because of the stigma associated with substance use, many don't confide in health professionals regarding their drug use. If you client is drinking excessive alcohol, explore when they last had some blood tests completed, particularly liver function tests. If the client injects drugs, or has done in the past, bloodborne virus screening is of upmost importance, to ensure early detection, prevention of transmission and treatment. Treatment available is greater than 95% effective for curing Hepatitis C[10]. It is not a requirement for a person to have stopped using drugs or drinking alcohol, to be treated for Hepatitis C.

Crisis management

Assisting the client to access resources and services to address their presenting crisis is important in building trust. Clients presenting as homeless or without their next meal, are not going to want to primarily talk about their drug use, however, will be motivated to explore ways to get a bed and a feed! Showing empathy and concern with the client's current situation builds therapeutic alliance.

It has been my experience, that focusing on the client's priority often results in opportunities to focus on their substance use. Sam, a 22-year-old man motivated to gain employment after losing his job, remained unmotivated to address his cannabis use. Sam had lost his job as a direct result of his cannabis use but was not ready to consider changing his drug use, or even to believe his drug use contributed to his unemployment. Our first two sessions mostly focused on strategies to search for a job, and the next steps to apply and prepare for an interview. Throughout

Permission

this process, Sam recognised that his cannabis use was a barrier for his success in both securing and sustaining a job.

Helen Mentha, psychologist and Motivational Interviewing trainer, encourages clinicians to spend the first 20% of time with the client simply deepening understanding of what the client is going through, suppressing the urge to give information or provide suggestions[11]. Motivational interviewing utilises the four communication skills known as OARS: open-ended questions, affirming, reflective listening, and summarising[12].

Application

Here is an example of a typical conversation with Sam, utilising OARS skills.

Sam: I just want to get another job; I need to be able to pay my bills. I'm sick of everyone harping on about me smoking weed. They all are boozers and I don't hassle them about it. If I don't smoke weed, I'm too anxious to work.
Tania: Working is really important to you. (affirming)
Sam: Yes, I have bills piling up, and it's making me even more anxious. And I'm smoking more weed than ever to cope.
Tania: It sounds like you need cannabis to manage your anxiety, which is out of control now because of your financial situation. (reflective listening)
Sam: Yeah, I'm smoking way too much. I'm never going to get a job smoking this much.
Tania: Smoking cannabis helps you manage your anxiety, and you feel that smoking gets in the way of you getting a job? (reflective listening)

Keep Calm and Treat Addiction

Sam: Yeah, I really need it to keep me calm, but it's stuffing up my life. I really need to figure out how to do life without it.
Tania: Cannabis has helped you with your anxiety up to this point and is now creating problems for you. You're ready to figure out another way to cope with your anxiety. (summarising)
Sam: I guess so, but I really don't know that it's possible…
Tania: It isn't surprising that you feel overwhelmed when thinking about change like this. I'm here to support you. Tell me about your priorities right now. (Affirming and open-ended question)

What started as a conversation with Sam not wanting to talk about changing his cannabis use, evolved to a conversation with Sam ready to consider change. Imagine the difference if rather than responding with the strengths-focused statement 'Working is really important to you', I had responded with 'Cannabis is really causing you some problems'. Sam would likely defend his cannabis use, possibly not engaging any further.

A common approach I utilise when the client presents denying any drug use, is to focus on their friends, or people they might know. Here is an example of a script:

'Even though you don't take ecstasy at festivals, you might have seen others around you doing it. Do you mind if I share with you some important ways to keep your friends, and others at the festival safe?' Once permission is granted, this is a great opportunity to share some harm minimisation tips. It is my experience, that because the conversation is now about other people, the client often asks questions and engages in the discussion.

Permission

You might be concerned that permitting the client to choose whether they use drugs or not, might keep them in precontemplation forever. The fact is, like anything else in life, drug use is a choice. Consequences are likely to follow at some point in time, such as broken relationships, deteriorating mental or physical health, legal implications and financial issues. Until these consequences outweigh the benefits the client is experiencing from their drug, it is unlikely they will move from precontemplation.

ACTION POINTS

- Have some information on hand to provide to your clients, particularly ways to minimise harm.

- Know where to send your clients for needle and syringe programs, and opioid treatment programs.

- Develop a better understanding of harm minimisation – check in on your own prejudices and beliefs. Are your conclusions evidence-based?

CHAPTER 10

Motivation

Everyone has inside of him a piece of good news. The good news is that you don't know how great you can be! How much you can love! What you can accomplish! And what your potential is!

Anne Frank

The contemplative stage of change presents an opportunity for the clinician to support the client moving forward into preparation and action, without directing them to do so. It is a time of possibility and hope for change. At this stage, the client is experiencing ambivalence; uncertainty as to whether their drug use is meeting their needs. Motivational Interviewing (MI) continues to be foundational to supporting the client at this stage, MI being founded by Miller and Rollnick in 2013, who described it as:

> *a collaborative goal-orientated style of communication with particular attention to the language of change. It is designed to strengthen personal motivation of, and commitment to a specific goal by eliciting and exploring the person's own reasons for change within an atmosphere of acceptance and compassion*[1].

An atmosphere of acceptance and compassion; sounds to me like a perfect environment to facilitate change! An environment without judgement, focusing on listening and understanding as the priority. In this chapter, we're going to explore why the stage of contemplation is so important, and how we as clinicians can best empower clients for change.

It's important in this stage to acknowledge both the benefits **and** the negative impacts of the substance use. The benefits identify why the client is trapped in this pattern of behaviour; there must be a payoff. Most people who are using substances are experiencing some positive benefits, otherwise, why would they keep doing it? Furthermore, it is essential to explore the negative impacts of the substance use, thereby identifying reasons for change, and the risks of not changing.

In the contemplative stage, choosing the right interventions and delivering these effectively as a clinician will support the person to move forward. It's going to tip the balance in the direction of change. At this time, the client often has low confidence in their ability to change. Remember, the client likely has lots of negative encouragers, and people supporting

Motivation

them to stay where they are. Potentially, they have tried many times to modify their behaviour in the past and been unable to sustain change. The clinician can be the positive voice, the person to inspire transformation through a collaborative, not authoritative partnership[2].

Although it may be enticing to rush change, don't underestimate the importance of sitting in the contemplation stage, strengthening the client's commitment to change. It's tempting as a clinician to try and push the client forward into preparation and action. However, contemplation provides the best environment to lay the foundation, establishing inconsistencies with current behaviour and your client's goals and values. It's an opportunity for the client to recognise good, solid evidence as to why they want and need change. The contemplation stage is the time for the clinician to strengthen self-efficacy of the client, by recognising strengths and past successes. Enhancing self-efficacy increases self-confidence, which is necessary to induce and sustain change.

Motivation is defined as:

> *a person's willingness to exert physical or mental effort in order to complete a goal or set aim*[3].

I hear it often said that the client lacks motivation, and this is just simply not true. Motivation is present in all of us; it's just a matter of channeling that motivation in the right direction.

Neglecting to identify or correctly address the contemplative stage results in a missed opportunity. Likewise, rushing a client through to preparation and action from contemplation is harmful, and can reinforce negative views on the possibility of change. When feeling pressured, the client is likely to start making arguments about change and defend their current position. If the clinician is experiencing discord with the client, this is not the client's fault! Commonly, these clients are labelled as resistant, combative and not ready for change. Resistance from the client is an indication that the clinician needs to change what they are doing; it is the mistake of the clinician's approach, not the fault of the client. At any sign of pushback from the client, the clinician needs to stop what they're doing, and move to some common ground to repair the therapeutic alliance[4].

Often, the contemplative stage is precipitated by hardship for the client. Some examples of this are: loss of licence due to drink driving, a health warning delivered by their GP, threatened loss of employment, or restrictions on access to their children. Maybe the client's partner has given them an ultimatum; stop using the drug or the relationship is over. Presenting in contemplation often means the client is presenting in a heightened state of anxiety over the consequences of their substance use. So, how do we best work with a client who is in the contemplative stage?

Cost-benefit analysis (CBA)

A CBA is a tool to weigh up the pros and cons to help decide on change. It is also known as a decisional balance. Talking through or writing up a CBA with the client is effective at this stage. The first step of the CBA process is acknowledging all the good things about using the drug.

Motivation

Some of the common benefits I hear from clients regarding their substance use include:

- an increase in confidence
- help in socialising
- relaxation aid
- anxiety reduction.

Identifying the benefits provides insight for future skills-building which may occur should the client progress to preparation and action phases. When completing a CBA, whilst it is important to first acknowledge the benefits of the drug use, most of the time should be spent on identifying the not so good things. Avoiding terminology of 'bad' or 'negative' also ensures the client isn't feeling like the clinician is making judgements about their use, facilitating an environment where it is entirely the client's responsibility to weigh up their drug use. I have often seen clients come to the realisation that they need and want to change their substance use, after hearing themselves identify the copious 'not so good' consequences of their drug use, compared to the minimal benefits.

It's important to only write down or acknowledge the benefits and not so good things that the client has identified. This is their list; it does not belong to the clinician or the family. For guidance in completing a CBA, be sure to see my free offer at the back of this book

> *There came a time when the risk to remain tight in the bud was more painful than the risk it took to blossom.*
>
> Anais Nin

The four Ls

When completing a CBA, I have often experienced clients not being able to think of not so good things about their drug use, even though it is obvious to everyone else! Employing a curious approach, utilising OARS skills is helpful in these circumstances. An effective framework I use to guide our discussion is an adaption of Roizen's 'four Ls' model[5]:

- Love
- Liver
- Livelihood
- Law.

Here is a table of examples of open-ended questions according to each domain:

The Four Ls	Open-ended questions
Love (partner, family, friends, relationships)	Was there a time when you noticed tension building in your relationship with your partner? Tell me what was happening.
Liver (physical health, mental health)	Tell me more about your depression and when you noticed it getting worse.
Livelihood (work, income, financial cost, study, hobbies)	What were the events leading up to your job loss?
Law (legal implications, drug testing at work)	How is probation going?

Motivation

Through exploring the four Ls, the client often recalls not so good things about their drug use. Although I often conduct cost-benefit analysis' verbally as part of my conversation with the client, having a visual of the CBA can be powerful. Seeing the long list of not so good consequences for their drug use beside a short list of benefits can be confronting for the client, and result in them identifying the need and desire to change. At this point, it is an important role of the clinician to listen and respond to change talk.

Change talk

When exploring the client's ambivalence, utilising the four Ls framework, listen for change talk used by the client and include it in your reflections. We can be reminded of preparatory and mobilising change talk by the DARN-CAT acronym. The following table describes the acronym, examples of change talk, and clinician reflection and elaboration[6].

Preparatory Change Talk	Examples	Reflection & elaboration
D (desire)	I **want** to stop using, I **wish** I could stop using, I would **like** to stop using, I **hope** to stop using	Making a change to your drug use is important to you. Tell me about a time in the past when you have made changes?

Keep Calm and Treat Addiction

Preparatory Change Talk	Examples	Reflection & elaboration
A (ability)	I **could** stop using, I **can** stop using, I **am able** to stop using	You are confident you can make a change to stop using. How will you go about it?
R (reason)	If I stop using my wife won't leave me	Saving your marriage is important to you. What would your relationship look like if you stopped using?
N (need)	I **need** to stop using, I **have to** stop using, I **must** stop using, it is so important to me to stop using, I've **got to** stop using, I **can't keep** using	You have decided you need to stop using. What do you think would happen if you didn't? On a scale of 0–10, how important is it for you to make this change?
Mobilising change talk	**Examples**	**Reflection & elaboration**
C (commitment)	I **am going** to change, I **will** change	You're determined to stop drinking this week. How can I support you with this plan?

Motivation

Preparatory Change Talk	Examples	Reflection & elaboration
A (activation)	I **am ready** to change, I **am willing** to change	You are ready to stop using. What will be your first step?
T (taking steps)	I have told my dealer to stop calling me	You've taken an important step in stopping your drug use. What else might support you to stop using?

By recognising mobilising change talk, and elaborating and reflecting, the clinician evokes commitment from the client. This is the key to helping clients move from their ambivalence, to preparing for action.

Application

Consider Sam, our 22-year-old man from the previous chapter, who was motivated to gain employment after losing his job. He has just identified cannabis as a barrier to securing and sustaining a job, and after the clinician's implementation of OARS techniques in the consult, Sam has demonstrated a shift from precontemplation to contemplation. Temptation arises for the clinician to leap into preparation and action, as Sam has expressed desire to change.

Keep Calm and Treat Addiction

Rather, by implementing a cost-benefit analysis utilising the four Ls framework, the clinician can further illicit commitment to change. Hearing himself talk about change, compels preparation and action for sustained change.

What if the clinician applies the CBA and four Ls, only for Sam to list copious good things about his cannabis use, unable to identify many not so good things? This is common and has happened in many of my sessions. In these cases, the client is likely not ready for change and is stuck in ambivalence. Chances are, they will swing between precontemplation and contemplation on a regular basis. This is completely normal.

Consider something in your own life that you have wanted to change; for example, maybe you have wanted, and indeed needed, to lose weight at some point. Can you recall spending a lot of time thinking about losing weight, even talking about it, and not **doing** anything about it (contemplator)? On some days, saying 'stuff it' and cracking open a family block of chocolate (happy user/precontemplator)? How would you feel if your GP pushed you into a plan to lose weight, when you knew in your heart that you were not ready to follow through with it? No doubt, you would crumple up that plan and throw it in the bin on the way out. Furthermore, you may not return to that GP again, in fear of him/her reprimanding you for not sticking to the plan. Change cannot be forced or rushed. If in doubt, progress as though your client is in precontemplation, listening for and evoking change talk wherever possible.

Consider that although there may be a lot listed in the good things' column, the items listed in the not so good column may outweigh them in importance. Sam might only have loss

Motivation

of his job listed in the not so good column, but his job and income is so important that it far outweighs any good thing about his cannabis use, and this motivates him for change. In these cases, skills-building is vitally important to ensure that the needs met by the drug (identified by the good things) are taken care of in alternative, healthy ways.

Maybe Sam doesn't want to spend time in contemplation, rather spring into action, and quit cannabis this week; that's fantastic! Work with him to complete a readiness for change ruler, helping identify his confidence in achieving change, and barriers to change[7]. Using a 1 to 10 scale (10 being the highest), Sam is asked to measure his confidence level for being able to successfully quit cannabis. Should Sam rate himself a 5, here are some suggested questions for exploration:

- What prevents you being a 6 or 7?
- What do you think you need to do to get yourself to a 6 or 7?

Sam may identify concerns about withdrawal or coping with anxiety, which can then be explored and addressed. He may identify that he needs to dispose of the remaining cannabis in his house, and this may be the first action identified to work toward his goal of quitting. It is helpful to encourage the client to complete a CBA as part of their homework, for reference in the future when tempted to lapse.

> *People often say that motivation doesn't last. Neither does bathing. That's why we recommend it daily.*
>
> Zig Ziglar

ACTION POINTS

- If you are not familiar with Motivational Interviewing, participate in some free online training. See Offer 1 at the back of this book for help with this.

- Become familiar with completing a cost-benefit analysis and download some worksheets. Consider practising in clinical supervision if you are lacking confidence, or even on your family members!

- 'Download and practise readiness for change rulers, and think about how you can implement them in your practice.

CHAPTER 11

Power

Success is the sum of small efforts, repeated day in and day out.

Robert Collier

Once ambivalence has been tipped in favour of change, the preparation and action phases begin. Preparation and action are times of determination, achievement, empowerment and self-discovery. Establishing a plan in the preparation phase encourages successful outcomes and supports the client to realise their goals. Preparation is the time to establish whether the client is seeking abstinence or moderation, and then defining short-term, smaller client-centred goals to support this destination. Regardless of what is expected of the client by friends, family or the law, setting realistic, achievable goals supports client success. The preparation stage lays the foundation for action; determining possible pitfalls and challenges that lay ahead. Skills and resources required are identified, providing a blueprint for therapy sessions in the action phase and beyond. The clinician and client address these gaps together, to support the client in reaching their goal.

Strengthening commitment to change continues to be valuable in the preparation stage. Persisting in the spirit of MI is vital, identifying and reflecting change talk as it arises. Self-doubt abounds in preparation; left unchecked, the client can feel overwhelmed and slip back into contemplation, or even precontemplation.

In the action phase, the client has begun to make changes, and is likely experiencing challenges in moving forward. For many, there has never been a time in their adult life where substance use hasn't played a significant role. Furthermore, there is likely both physical and emotional effects of withdrawal to address.

The brain's prefrontal lobe is still developing until our early twenties. Formulating plans, discernment, making choices, regulating impulsiveness and language are all important functions supported by the prefrontal lobe. It's important to remember this when working with clients who have used a lot of substances in their younger years, as this can impact the client's ability to set goals and problem solve[1].

Fortunately, modern science has discovered neuroplasticity of the brain, which means the brain can learn and create new pathways; it is not fixed and inflexible[2]. This means that with brain training through therapy, there is hope that unhelpful neural pathways formed in the early years by drugs and alcohol can be replaced with healthy ones[3]. Brain retraining requires persistence and repetition to be successful, emphasising the need for these clients to remain in therapeutic treatment for a period of time to sustain change.

Inadequate attention to goal setting and planning puts the client in a precarious situation where they are unlikely to commit to their recovery plan. Hastily deciding on unrealistic goals sets the client up for disappointment and feeds into their negative self-talk derived from unsuccessful past attempts at change. The action phase requires focus, and commitment of time and energy to address the skill gaps that have been identified in the preparation.

When the past calls, let it go to voicemail. Believe me, it has nothing new to say.

Unknown

Goal setting

Most important is setting some SMART goals: specific, measurable, achievable, realistic and time related. Ensure the plan is the client's plan, and they are deciding on a goal they are ready to commit to. Goals are best broken down to smaller ones, that can be achieved before the next appointment. Often the first goals set don't involve any change in drug use; they are simply laying the foundation for future change.[4] The following table breaks down some areas that often need

Keep Calm and Treat Addiction

attention when addressing substance use and suggests some commonly identified SMART goals.

Problem	SMART goal
Environment • living with other users • homeless • unsupportive environment	In the next seven days I will ring six residential rehab facilities and put my name on the waiting list. I will always ensure that I keep my phone with me and answer all calls even if they are from private numbers.
Resources • medications for physical withdrawal/ cravings • benchmarking	I will attend my GP appointment tomorrow for a medical check to discuss reducing alcohol. I will keep a drinking diary for the next seven days to monitor and be more mindful of my drinking and will bring it to my next session for discussion.
Triggers • social media • mobile phone	Today I will deactivate my Facebook account. I will discard my SIM card and drug-related contacts and buy a new SIM card with a new phone number.
Supply • dealers • mates	I will talk to my workmates tomorrow and tell them I have decided to reduce drinking on the advice of my GP. I will ask them for their support in improving my health. I will take zero alcohol beer to after work drinks on Friday.

Power

Obstacles and supports

Looking forward to the week ahead and recognising potential obstacles to meeting recovery goals is crucial. Once identified, the clinician and client can work together to problem-solve strategies supportive of a positive outcome.

Here are a couple of examples of frequently identified obstacles and subsequent strategies:

Obstacle	Strategy
Wednesday will be a stressful day at work.	• Practice mindfulness • Meet a friend after work • Book another counselling session for Wednesday afternoon • Go to bed early on Tuesday night
Thursday is pay day.	• Give bank card to trusted partner/family member • Shop for food, essentials and pay all bills with support person on Thursday
The kids are at their dad's on the weekend and I am always lonely.	• Make appointments with friends/family • Challenge unhelpful thoughts • Create a pamper weekend • Volunteer in the community

Likewise, support the client to pinpoint supportive people and practices that have assisted with change in the past.

- Perhaps last time they moderated or quit, SMART Recovery or Alcoholics Anonymous was central to their success – would they consider joining again?
- Is there a hobby that they used to enjoy, but have let go as a result of their substance use – can they restart it?
- Did their GP prescribe antidepressants, but they have never filled the script – would they consider starting the medication?
- Have spiritual practices helped in the past – can they reconnect?

Eating a healthy diet, drinking plenty of water, and participating in daily exercise are all ways the client can support their recovery. Frequently, healthy habits and routines are the first to go when substance use increases. Likewise, re-establishing healthy sleep routines by implementing good sleep hygiene practices assists healing.

Skills building

When identifying potential obstacles, it is likely that skills gaps are detected, such as mindfulness and recognising unhelpful thoughts listed in the table above.

This is a list of examples of further skills that are commonly identified in my practice as helpful to supporting the client be successful in achieving their substance-related goals:

- managing cravings and triggers
- lapse and relapse prevention and management

Power

- distress tolerance
- values-based living
- building a healthy self-esteem
- anger management
- managing anxiety and depression
- coping with stress
- dealing with past trauma
- maintaining healthy relationships
- assertive communication
- problem solving
- sleep hygiene
- pain management.

Hopefully this list clarifies with you that working with addiction is no different to much of the work you do with your clients. The majority of work done with clients using substances isn't about drugs at all, rather working on the skills supporting the client's ability to cope with life's challenges, instead of relying on a substance for immediate relief.

Following is a list of evidence-based therapeutic interventions shown to be valuable in AOD services[5]:

- contingency management
- cognitive behavioural therapy
- narrative therapy
- mindfulness
- motivational enhancement/interviewing
- solution focused therapy
- emotional regulation therapy
- acceptance and commitment therapy
- dialectical behavioural therapy

- art/music therapy
- exercise and healthy lifestyle programs.

Application

Sam, aged 22 from the previous chapters, presents to you ready to spring into action and quit cannabis this week. He has identified himself as a 5 out of 10 in confidence level and is adamant that his goal is to not smoke cannabis again – as of now! The reason he provides for scoring himself as a 5 and not higher, is that he lives in a share house where all his friends smoke together every evening. As his clinician, it is obvious to you that this goal is unrealistic because of his environment, and likely to end in disappointment. However, no amount of MI and reflective conversation will bring Sam to this realisation, and he is determined to forge ahead with the goal.

It is my experience that clients often set unrealistic goals and are unwilling to budge from these. Sometimes it takes time for the client to learn from trial and error, that it is better to approach their long-term goals from a different angle. This is the journey of change; when Sam returns, potentially unsuccessful in his goal to cease cannabis, the clinician can reflect on this with Sam, identifying the barriers and triggers and how these can be addressed.

Another possible scenario is Sam not returning at all to further therapeutic sessions after his goal-setting session. There can be various reasons for this; I have listed below common reasons clients have disengaged from my experience:

Power

- motivation when presenting at time of crisis has waned now the crisis has passed
- embarrassment due to not following through with the plan discussed
- they have succeeded with the plan and don't want further help.

At the conclusion of sessions, it is important to emphasise the importance of continuing in therapy, despite the outcomes of the week. Accentuate that there is no judgement on the part of the clinician, and that we all struggle with change. It is helpful to show the client a diagram of the stages of change, normalising the process.

> *Tomorrow is the most important thing in life. Comes into us at midnight very clean. It's perfect when it arrives and it puts itself in our hands. It hopes we've learned something from yesterday.*
>
> John Wayne

ACTION POINTS

- Add some goal setting templates to your AOD toolbox.

- Ensure you have worksheets and resources at hand for skills building.

- Create a list of other service providers who can provide support in the areas you are not confident or skilled in.

CHAPTER 12

Breakthrough

Our greatest glory is not in never failing, but in rising up every time we fail.

Ralph Waldo Emerson

After sustaining the action phase for some time, and upholding their goal, the client progresses to maintenance. The maintenance stage is characterised by the client reaching a new normal, no longer constantly battling cravings and triggers to sustain their goals. In my experience, clients are impeded from reaching maintenance if they haven't engaged actively in skills building when accessing support in the previous stages. Achieving maintenance is valuable because missing out on maintenance, equates to missing out on benefits and positive consequences of the difficult changes that have been endured. In action, clients encounter a difficult battle, yet fail to experience full victory where the benefits of making these changes can be enjoyed completely. Failing to reach maintenance is like quitting a university degree with only one subject left and never graduating!

In maintenance, clients often begin to reap rewards such as repaired relationships, improved health and better finances. Although maintenance is a time to enjoy the spoils of hard work, it isn't a time to be complacent. Lapses and relapses can occur at any stage in the change cycle, as indicated by the diagram of the Stages of Change at the start of Part C. Some clients tell me that they feel more at risk of lapsing in maintenance, because they aren't focused day-to-day on sustaining their changes, and can get caught out by unexpected challenges. Specifically, reaching milestones can be triggering. Clients often say that attaining and passing a sobriety milestone can intensify cravings. For example, a client who has abstained from alcohol for a maximum of 12 months in the past, feels increased cravings and desires to drink on passing this sobriety marker. Acknowledging these triggering dates and preparing for challenges that may arise as a result equip the client to sustain their goals.

Research indicates that relapses are a normal experience for those working on behaviour change, particularly related to substance use[1]. Relapse prevention and planning is of vital importance for the lifelong journey ahead. The longer a person can continue in change, the more likely it will endure[2]. Adequate relapse prevention training, inclusive of management of lapses and relapses increases the likelihood of permanent change. This knowledge, along with the skill of managing cravings and triggers, is recommended to be acquired in the action phase.

After a lapse or relapse, it is common for clients to avoid re-engaging with services because of shame. As emphasised last chapter, it is critical that the clinician communicates an open door, no failure policy with the client. Life isn't smooth sailing for anyone; there will be problems and adversities and making mistakes is a normal part of life. Resilience is built when lessons are learnt from these mistakes, obstacles are overcome, and the client is equipped for the next hurdle life brings. Hiding any slip-ups from family, friends and support services often intensifies the shame, resulting in further decline.

Naturally, by the time the client reaches the maintenance stage, engagement with counselling is sporadic, if happening at all. It is important for the client to have plans for easy access to supports when needed. Relapse prevention builds the capacity of the client to stay in maintenance[3]. In this chapter, we're going to identify risk factors for relapse, and will explore management of lapses, empowering the client to avoid relapse and sustain their maintenance.

High-risk situations

Relapse prevention planning involves identifying high-risk situations and triggers that increase vulnerability to using substances. The clinician can work with the client to explore lapses in the past and identify common triggers and high-risk situations contributing to substance use. Triggers can be classified into two groups: external and internal[4]. The following table provides some examples of internal and external triggers, and high-risk situations.

Internal trigger	External trigger	High-risk situations
Negative emotions such as anger, sadness, anxiety, boredom, guilt, stress, loneliness, disappointment, fear	Arguments and relationship stressors, loss of a loved one	Special occasions and celebrations, e.g. birthdays, Christmas
Positive emotions such as excitement, happiness, satisfaction, pride, love, elation	Peer pressure	Overconfidence, or underestimating the risk of the situation
Being tired, not getting enough sleep, being in physical pain	Familiar location of drug use	The end of a day at work, Friday afternoons, the weekend, payday
Feeling energetic	Pressure at work, loss of a job	After mowing the lawn

Recognising emotions, triggers, or high-risk situations that increase vulnerability to a lapse can alert the client and provide opportunity to intervene and seek support. By identifying high-risk situations and triggers that may be arising in the coming week, the clinician can assist the client to be confident with strategies to overcome these challenges.

Breakthrough

The following list provides examples of strategies that can be utilised prior to a lapse to help stay on track:

- call a support person, counsellor, friend, help line
- get active
- attend a self-help group
- perform relaxation techniques
- read completed cost benefit analysis worksheet
- leave the situation or environment
- come up with a plan for the high-risk situation before getting there, or avoid altogether
- distract with another activity.

Being alert for early warning signs of a lapse can provide an opportunity to intervene early, rather than waiting for the craving to take hold. Some examples of early warning signs are moodiness, self-isolating, changes to sleep (either more or sleeplessness), changes in appetite or not attending to daily responsibilities. The sooner intervention occurs, the more successful the client will be in deterring the substance use.

Lapse

A lapse is a slip-up; the client initially attains their objective of abstinence or moderation, but then makes a mistake by using once, or more often than they had planned[5]. Susan, aged 42, has maintained her goal of abstinence from cigarettes for six months. Susan identifies drinking alcohol as a high-risk situation for a lapse, but she feels confident that after six months of abstinence, a few drinks will not be a problem. While enjoying a night out with friends, she smokes five cigarettes.

Keep Calm and Treat Addiction

If things go wrong, don't go with them.
Roger Babson

Susan wakes up the next morning feeling angry at herself and rings her counsellor in tears. Essential points to highlight in this conversation with Susan include:

- *Strengths.* Susan has only smoked five cigarettes, not a whole packet, and she has woken up today and not smoked any more. Instead, Susan has reached out for help by calling her counsellor.

- *Moving forward.* What can Susan do today to ensure she moves forward to continue in maintenance. An example might be revising her craving management strategies and practising them when she feels like a cigarette.

- *Learnings.* On reflection, what can Susan do differently if faced with the same situation, to maintain her abstinence? Susan might identify that next time she will talk to her friends prior to going out and ask them not to offer her cigarettes. Susan might recognise that she needs to stay sober enough to enable sound decision making.

Although lapses are not to be viewed as failures, they are not void of consequences. Susan is likely to experience increased nicotine cravings as a result of her lapse. It may be necessary for her to re-engage with support to revisit some of the skills useful for managing increased cravings and triggers. For clients using other substances, there can be harsher consequences such as damaged relationships and legal implications as a result of a lapse. Accessing counselling and support is critical to ensure the client does not deteriorate to relapse.

Relapse

Relapse is signified by regression to the precontemplative or contemplative stage, returning to preceding patterns of substance use behaviour[3]. Should Susan have woken up the following day, and upon discovering the remainder of a packet of cigarettes in her jacket pocket, smoked the rest of them while drinking coffee and engaging in unhelpful thinking, chances are she would have spiraled into a relapse. Most commonly, Susan's self-talk at this time would have sounded something like this:

> *'I am hopeless and weak. I've really stuffed up now, so many people are going to be disappointed in me, I've let everyone down. What's the point, I've got no willpower, I'm never gonna quit cigarettes.'*

Perceiving a slip-up as a total failure, is known as the abstinence violation effect[1]. This thinking pattern is commonly followed by feelings of shame and guilt, resulting in relapse. Challenging unhelpful thinking styles and replacing with healthier alternatives supports the client to self-correct lapses and sustain maintenance.

Application

Simon, aged 35, has addressed his alcohol dependence for the first time and has been abstinent for four weeks. He is already feeling the benefits of his behaviour change: better sleep, enhanced mood and improved relationship with his wife. Upon raising the importance of relapse prevention, Simon becomes defensive, almost insulted that the clinician believes he will drink again. I have encountered many clients who, like Simon, are adamant that they don't need relapse prevention, as there is no chance they will ever return to their substance use. Unfortunately, such clients often return following a relapse.

Relapse prevention plans can be likened to car insurance. When a person insures a car, it is not in the expectation that the car will be in an accident. Rather, it is a backup plan, should the unfortunate incident occur and the car need repairing. Having car insurance does not give the driver permission to have an accident. No-one sets out to have a car accident because insurance has been purchased. There are consequences to using the insurance, such as physical injury, an excess to pay and increased premiums as a result of the claim. However, car insurance enables the person to recover more quickly from accidents, financing the repair so that the car can get back on the road. Employing this narrative to frame the role of a relapse prevention plan can reassure the client and improve their understanding of its importance.

When Simon engages again after relapse and gets back on track, he may be ready to discuss a relapse prevention plan. Relapse prevention plans reinforce lapses as a normal part of

Breakthrough

recovery, and an opportunity to learn from the mistake in order to prevent relapses and to strengthen future recovery.

Relapse prevention plans consider the following:

- learnings from previous lapses
- what led up to the lapse
- what helped get back on track
- what increases vulnerability to a lapse
- are there warning signs of a lapse
- what are interventions if the signs are recognised
- what will help get back on track
- who can I contact?

Though no-one can go back and make a brand new start, anyone can start from now and make a brand new ending.
                                                        Carl Bard

ACTION POINTS

- Include a copy of a Relapse Prevention Plan in your AOD toolbox.

- Promote peer support groups (both face to face and online) such as SMART Recovery to support ongoing maintenance.

- Want to dig deeper? Engage in online learning to upskill in AOD knowledge. Email tania@taniakellyhealth.com.au to request access to free resources.

Afterword

Congratulations on completing the book, and equipping yourself with the evidence-based information needed to support your clients on their recovery journey.

In Part A, we firstly explored the fundamentals of addiction treatment, remembering that the client is the expert in their recovery journey – you don't have to wear that hat! Addiction treatment is something that needs to be planned and is best not rushed, and it doesn't define who the client is. Addiction is a symptom, not an identity. Also, not everyone who uses substances needs treatment; there is a spectrum of use.

Secondly in Part B, we identified the options for treatment. Abstinence and moderation were considered, detox and rehab were defined. There is not a one size fits all response to addiction treatment, it is important to help your client identify what is right for them. We discussed the myth of rock bottom, and the dangers of this principle.

Keep Calm and Treat Addiction

Finally, in Part C the Stages of Change Model was examined, identifying interventions applicable to where your client is at. The precontemplator is the happy user, not ready for change. The contemplater is considering change, however, benefits of substance use are keeping them stuck. The person in preparation and action is moving forward, making plans and changes towards recovery. And the person in maintenance is enjoying the 'new normal', not having to battle thoughts of substance use as often as they used to, starting to reap the rewards of a new lifestyle. Of course, throughout this journey is the risk of lapse or relapse, which is considered a reality of recovery rather than a failure. The learnings from these lapses and relapses can further strengthen the recovery journey.

So, as you *Keep Calm and Treat Addiction*, this book now becomes your go-to guide. Got a client in precontemplation – take yourself straight to Chapter 9 as a reminder of how to best support them at this stage. Got family members talking about rock bottom – remind yourself of the reason this mindset is risky by heading straight to Chapter 8. And of course, you have all your location-specific resources that you have identified whilst working through the chapters.

Addiction is tough, and supporting someone experiencing addiction is not easy. Thank you for caring enough to read this book and be sure to access your free resources to equip you in your journey ahead.

About the Author

Tania Kelly, was born in Mount Isa, in outback Queensland, but was raised on the coast in Bundaberg. In 2009, Tania, her husband Paul and their three children moved to Mackay, in beautiful North Queensland. They now call themselves locals and enjoy exploring the many natural environments of this amazing part of Australia they live in.

As a Mental Health Nurse and Tobacco Treatment Specialist, Tania has experience in facilitating both face to face and online groups. She holds a Postgraduate Diploma in Mental Health Nursing and is an authorised SMART Recovery Facilitator. Tania's diverse nursing career started in 1989 and has included peri-operative, community, general practice, nursing education, adolescent health, project management, mental health and addiction nursing. In 2013 she discovered a passion for supporting people in their mental health and addiction journeys. This has let to the establishment of her own

Keep Calm and Treat Addiction

nurse-led clinic, Tania Kelly Health Consultant in Mackay. In addition to private practice, her counselling experience spans across a variety of treatment environments inclusive of inpatient, outreach and community-based settings.

As a senior clinician, Tania constantly shares the concepts outlined in this book with health service providers. Tania wants to demystify addiction treatment, and equip others inclusive of psychologists, social workers, nurses, doctors, allied health professionals, counsellors, youth workers, support workers and chaplains (to name a few) to feel confident in working with their current client base who are struggling with addiction. Ultimately, it is Tania's desire to increase the access of evidence-based support for those struggling with addiction.

Tania can be emailed on tania@taniakellyhealth.com.au

Visit her website at www.taniakellyhealth.com.au

Call her on 0428 480 295

Reference List

Chapter 1

1. ADF. (2019). Stigma and people who use drugs. Retrieved from https://adf.org.au/insights/stigma-people-who-use-drugs/
2. Hallam, K. (n.d.). The therapeutic alliance stays strong. Retrieved from https://www.nada.org.au/resources/publications/therapeutic-alliance-stays-strong/
3. Qld Health. (2016). Connecting care to recovery 2016–2021. Retrieved from https://www.health.qld.gov.au/__data/assets/pdf_file/0020/465131/connecting-care.pdf
4. Insight. (2016). Qld AOD treatment service delivery framework. Retrieved from https://insight-prod.s3.ap-southeast-2.amazonaws.com/public/guidelines/1511825138_statewide-framewrk-compre-care.pdf
5. Turning Point. (2018). Drug and alcohol withdrawal guidelines. https://www.turningpoint.org.au/sites/default/files/inline-files/Alcohol-and-Drug-Withdrawal-Guidelines-2018.pdf

Chapter 2

1. Moos, R., & Moos, B. (2006). Rates and predictors of relapse after natural and treated remission from alcohol use disorders. Addiction, 101(2), 212–222. https://doi.org/10.1111/j.1360-0443.2006.01310.x
2. Daley, D., & Douaihy, A. (2015). Relapse prevention counselling: Clinical strategies to guide addiction recovery and reduce relapse. Retrieved from http://search.ebscohost.com/login.aspx?direct=true&AuthType=sso&db=nlebk&AN=1055375&scope=site&authtype=sso&custid=s3716178&ebv=EB&ppid=pp_xiii
3. Macatee, R., Albanese, B., Crane, N., Okey, S., Cougle, J., & Schmidt, N. (2018). Distress intolerance moderation of neurophysiological markers of response inhibition after induced stress: Relations with cannabis use disorder. Psychology of Addictive Behaviors, 32(8), 944–955. https://doi.org/10.1037/adb0000418.supp
4. Rosen, R. (2019) Distress intolerance and withdrawal severity among daily smokers: The role of smoking abstinence expectancies. Addictive behaviors, 99, ISSN: 0306-4603 Online ISSN: 1873-6327
5. Luberto, C., McLeish, A., Robertson, S., Avallone, K., Kraemer, K., & Jeffries, E. (2014). The role of mindfulness skills in terms of distress tolerance: A pilot test among adult daily smokers. The American Journal on Addictions, 23(2), 184–188. https://doi.org/10.1111/j.1521-0391.2013.12096.x
6. Selbekk, A., & Sagvaag, H. (2016). Troubled families and individualised solutions: An institutional discourse analysis of alcohol and drug treatment practices involving affected others. Sociology of Health & Illness, 38(7), 1058–1073. https://doi.org/10.1111/1467-9566.12432

Reference List

Chapter 3

1. Robinson, S. (2017). 'Alcoholic' or 'Person with alcohol use disorder'? Applying person-first diagnostic terminology in the clinical domain. Substance abuse, 38(1), 9–14 http://dx.doi.org/10.1080/08897077.2016.1268239
2. Kelly J., & Westerhoff, C. (2010). Does it matter how we refer to individuals with substance-related conditions? A randomized study of two commonly used terms. International Journal of Drug Policy, 21(3), 202–7. doi:10.1016/j.drugpo.2009.10.010.
3. Bradshaw, S. D., Shumway, S. T., Dsauza, C. M., Morris, N., & Haynes, N. D. (2017). Hope, coping skills, and the prefrontal cortex in alcohol use disorder recovery. American Journal of Drug & Alcohol Abuse, 43(5), 591–601. doi: 10.1080/00952990.2017.1286500.
4. Department of Health, Australia. (2019). National alcohol strategy 2019–2028. Retrieved from https://apo.org.au/node/270691
5. Strong, T., & Pyle, N. (2009). Constructing a conversational 'miracle': Examining the 'miracle question' as it is used in therapeutic dialogue. Journal of Constructivist Psychology, 22(4), 328–353. https://doi.org/10.1080/10720530903114001
6. Bradshaw, S., Shumway, S. T., Wang, E. W., Harris, K. S., Smith, D. B., & Austin Robillard, H. (2015). Hope, readiness, and coping in family recovery from addiction. Journal of Groups in Addiction & Recovery, 10(4), 313–336. https://doi.org/10.1080/1556035X.2015.1099125
7. Insight, Qld Health. (2019). Micro-counselling skills. Retrieved from https://insight.qld.edu.au

8. Mentha, H. (2018). MI spirit in action. [electronic mailing list message]
9. Hayes, S. C., Wilson, K. G., Gifford, E. V., Bissett, R., Piasecki, M., Batten, S. V., Byrd, M., & Gregg, J. (2004). A preliminary trial of twelve-step facilitation and acceptance and commitment therapy with polysubstance-abusing methadone-maintained opiate addicts. Behaviour Therapy 35, 667–688. Retrieved from https://www.actmindfully.com.au/upimages/Kelly_Wilson_ACT_substance_abuse.pdf
10. Frings, D., Wood, K., Lionetti, N., & Albery, I. (2019). Tales of hope: Social identity and learning lessons from others in Alcoholics Anonymous: A test of the Social Identity Model of Cessation Maintenance. Addictive Behaviors, 93, 204-211.

Chapter 4

1. Fairchild. A., Bayer. B., & Colgrove, J. (2015). Risky business: New York City's experience with fear-based public health campaigns. Health Affairs, 34(5): 844-851. does: 10.1377/hlthaff.2014.1236
2. Williamson, B. (2017). ABC Radio Adelaide: Ice epidemic media coverage creating unnecessary fear, drug expert says. Retrieved from https://www.abc.net.au/news/2017-02-15/drug-professor-nicole-lee-says-ice-epidemic-not-true/8272742
3. Australian Institute of Health & Welfare. (2017). National drug strategy household survey 2016. Retrieved from https://www.aihw.gov.au/getmedia/15db8c15-7062-4cde-bfa4-3c2079f30af3/21028a.pdf.aspx?inline=true

Reference List

4. International Network of People Who Use Drugs. (n.d.). Timeline of events in the history of drugs. Retrieved from https://inpud.wordpress.com/timeline-of-events-in-the-history-of-drugs/
5. The Centre for YouthAOD Practice Development. (n.d.). YouthAOD toolbox: Patterns of use. Retrieved from https://www.youthaodtoolbox.org.au/patterns-use-0
6. Turton, S., & Lingford-Hughes, A. (2016). Neurobiology and principles of addiction and tolerance. Medicine, 44(12), 693-696.
7. World Health Organization. (2010). The Alcohol, Smoking and Substance Involvement Screening Test (ASSIST): Manual for use in primary care. Retrieved from https://www.who.int/substance_abuse/publications/assist/en/

Chapter 5

1. Australian Drug Foundation. (2020). Withdrawal. Retrieved from https://adf.org.au/reducing-risk/withdrawal/
2. National Health and Medical Research Council. (2020). Australian guidelines to reduce health risks from drinking alcohol. Retrieved from https://www.nhmrc.gov.au/health-advice/alcohol

Chapter 6

1. American Addiction Centers Resource. Alcohol withdrawal kindling effects.
Retrieved from https://www.alcohol.org/effects/kindling-withdrawal/

2. Australian Drug Foundation. (2020). Withdrawal. Retrieved from https://adf.org.au/reducing-risk/withdrawal/
3. Lee, M. T., Torres, M., Brolin, M., Merrick, E. L., Ritter, G. A., Panes, L., Horgan, C. M., Lane, N., Hopwood, J. C., De Marco, N., & Gewirtz, A. (2020). Impact of recovery support navigators on continuity of care after detoxification. Journal of Substance Abuse Treatment, 112, 10-16.
4. Turning Point. (2018). Drug and alcohol withdrawal guidelines. Retrieved from https://www.turningpoint.org.au/sites/default/files/inline-files/Alcohol-and- Drug Withdrawal-Guidelines-2018.pdf
5. Schultz, N. R., Martinez, R., Cucciare, M. A., & Timko, C. (2016). Patient, program, and system barriers and facilitators to detoxification services in the U.S. veterans health administration: A qualitative study of provider perspectives. Substance Use & Misuse, 51(10), 1330–1341. https://doi.org/10.3109/10826084.2016.1168446
6. NSW Government. (n.d.) The hospital drug and alcohol consultation liaison model of care. Retrieved from https://www.health.nsw.gov.au/aod/professionals/Pages/hosp-DA-consult-moc.aspx
7. Mager, D. (2015). Detoxing after detox: The perils of post-acute withdrawal. Retrieved from https://www.psychologytoday.com/us/blog/some-assembly-required/201505/detoxing-after-detox-the-perils-post-acute-withdrawal

Chapter 7

1. Choolabi, M. O., Moloodi, R., Ahounbar, E., Taremian, F., & Farhadi, M. H. (2018). Relapse among patients referring

Reference List

to residential rehabilitation centers for drug use disorders in Iran and its related factors. Iranian Rehabilitation Journal, 16(2),139-146
2. Lee, N. (2018). The conversation: Drug rehab: What works and what to keep in mind when choosing a private treatment provider. Retrieved from https://www.abc.net.au/news/2018-05-02/drug-rehab-what-works-and-what-to-keep-in-mind-when-choosing/9718124
3. Drink and Drug News. (n.d.) A new dayhab treatment centre sets out to make recovery available to everyone who needs it. Retrieved from https://drinkanddrugsnews.com/dayhab-drug-treatment-help-me-stop/

Chapter 8

1. Trimingham, T. (2009). Not my family; never my child. Allen & Unwin, NSW.
2. Family Drug Support and Qld Injectors Health Network. (2007). A guide to coping: Support for families faced with problematic drug use. FDS: NSW
3. Selva, J. (2020). How to set healthy boundaries. Retrieved from https://positivepsychology.com/great-self-care-setting-healthy-boundaries/
4. Family Drug Support Australia. (n.d.). Setting boundaries. Retrieved from https://fds.org.au/table/coping-tips/setting-boundaries/
5. Carpenter, K. M., Foote, J., Hedrick, T., Collins, K., & Clarkin, S. (2019). Building on shared experiences: The evaluation of a phone-based parent-to-parent support program for helping parents with their child's substance misuse. Addictive Behaviors, Jan2020(100), 106103.

6. Family Drug Support Australia. (n.d.). Coping tips: Conflict and substance abuse.
   Retrieved from https://fds.org.au/dealing-with-conflict/conflict-and-substance-abuse
7. Department of Health, Cracks in the Ice. (n.d.). How to protect yourself and others. Retrieved from https://cracksintheice.org.au/families-friends/how-to-protect-yourself-and-others
8. Wilson, S., Lubman, D. I., Rodda, S., Manning, V., & Yap, M. (2018). The personal impacts of having a partner with problematic alcohol or other drug use: Descriptions from online counselling sessions. Addiction Research & Theory, 26(4), 315-322.
9. Trimingham, T. (n.d.). Family drug support online: Walking the tightrope. [video].
   Retrieved from https://www.fdsonline.org.au/

Part C

1. Gold, M. (2020). Stages of change. Retrieved from https://psychcentral.com/lib/stages-of-change/

Chapter 9

1. Krebs, P., Norcross, J. C., Nicholson, J. M., & Prochaska, J. O. (2018). Stages of change and psychotherapy outcomes: A review and meta-analysis. Journal of Clinical Psychology, 74(11), 1964–1979. https://doi.org/10.1002/jclp.22683
2. Australian Government Department of Health. (2004). What is harm minimisation?

Reference List

Retrieved from https://www1.health.gov.au/internet/publications/publishing.nsf/Content/drugtreatpubs-front5-wk-toc~drugtreat-pubs-front5-wk-secb~drugtreat-pubs-front5-wk-secb-6~drugtreat-pubs-front5-wk-secb-6-1

3. Harm Reduction Australia. (2018). What is harm reduction? Retrieved from https://www.harmreductionaustralia.org.au/what-is-harm-reduction/
4. Queensland Health. (2018). Queensland needle and syringe program. Retrieved From https://www.health.qld.gov.au/public-health/topics/atod/queensland-needle-syringe-program
5. Clinical Excellence Division. (2018). Queensland medication-assisted treatment of opioid dependence: Clinical guidelines 2018. Retrieved from https://adis.health.qld.gov.au/sites/default/files/resource/file/qld-matod-clin-gdln-2018.pdf
6. Pill Testing Australia. (2019). Retrieved from https://pilltestingaustralia.com.au/
7. Deakin University. (n.d.). How safe injecting rooms will benefit the community.
Retrieved from https://this.deakin.edu.au/society/should-we-introduce-safe-injecting-rooms
8. Larney, S. (2017). A global picture of injecting drug use, HIV and anti-HCV Prevalence among people who inject drugs, and coverage of harm reduction interventions. Retrieved from http://connections.edu.au/researchfocus/global-picture-injecting-drug-use-hiv-and-anti-hcv-prevalence-among-people-who-inject
9. The Centre for Youth AOD Practice Development. (n.d.). Engaging clients under coercion. Retrieved from https://www.youthaodtoolbox.org.au/12-engaging-clients-under-coercion
10. Hepatitis Australia. (2019). Preventing hepatitis C. Retrieved from https://www.hepatitisaustralia.com/hepatitis-c-prevention

11. Mentha, H. (2018). Empathy in action. [electronic mailing list message].
12. Souders, B. (2020). 17 motivational interviewing questions and skills. Retrieved from https://positivepsychology.com/motivational-interviewing/

Chapter 10

1. Miller, W. R., & Rollnick, S. (2013) Motivational Interviewing: Helping people to change (3rd Edition). Guilford Press.
2. Hall, K., Gibbie, T., & Lubman, D. (2012). Motivational interviewing techniques: Facilitating behaviour change in the general practice setting. Psychological strategies 41(9), 660-667.
3. Pam, N. (2013). Motivation. Retrieved from www.psychologydictionary.org/motivation/
4. Westra, H. A., & Norouzian, N. (2018). Using motivational interviewing to manage process markers of ambivalence and resistance in cognitive behavioral therapy. Cognitive Therapy and Research, 42(2), 193–203. https://doi.org/10.1007/s10608-017-9857-6
5. Insight. (2019). 4 L's Worksheet. Retrieved from https://insight.qld.edu.au/shop/4-ls-worksheet
6. Waitt, A. (n.d.). Change talk. Retrieved from https://my.ireta.org/sites/ireta.org/files/Cultivating%20Change%20Talk%20-%20without%20video.pdf
7. Royal College of Nursing UK. (2019). Readiness to change. Retrieved from https://www.rcn.org.uk/clinical-topics/supporting-behaviour-change/readiness-to-change

Reference List

Chapter 11

1. Mental Health Commission. (n.d.). Impact of alcohol on the developing brain. Retrieved from www.alcoholthinkagain.com.au
2. Malcom, L. (2015). Neuroplasticity: how the brain can heal itself. Retrieved from https://www.abc.net.au/radionational/programs/allinthemind/neuroplasticity-and-how-the-brain-can-heal-itself/6406736
3. Dovetail. (2020). Neuroplasticity – Dots and the brain. [video]. Retrieved from https://insight.qld.edu.au/training/neuroplasticity-dots-and-the-brain/detail
4. Healthdirect. (2018). Goal setting. Retrieved from https://www.healthdirect.gov.au/goal-setting
5. Queensland Health (2016). Alcohol and other drugs therapeutic intervention overview. Retrieved from https://insight-prod.s3.ap-southeast-2.amazonaws.com/public/guidelines/1571044076_revised-poster-3-alcohol-and-other-drugs-therapeutic-intervention-overview-21pdf.pdf

Chapter 12

1. Insight. (2019). Relapse prevention and management. Retrieved from https://insight.qld.edu.au/training
2. Hochman, D. (2019). Self-recovery: Maintenance, stages of change series. Retrieved from https://www.selfrecovery.org/blog/maintenance/
3. The Centre for YouthAOD Practice Development. (n.d.). What is relapse prevention? Retrieved from https://www.youthaodtoolbox.org.au/what-relapse-prevention

4. Turning Point. (2019). Keep going: How to move on from relapse. Retrieved from https://www.counsellingonline.org.au/blog/how-to-move-on-from-relapse
5. National Centre for Education & Training on Addiction. (2020). Relapse prevention and management. Retrieved from http://nceta.flinders.edu.au/

OFFER 1

Keep calm and download your free resources

Download your FREE Keep Calm and Treat Addiction resources to assist you in applying the action points from each chapter in your practice. With free membership to this secret webpage, you will have lifetime access to all of my resources, ensuring you have the worksheets and tools at your fingertips to support your clients. This webpage is maintained regularly, giving you access to the latest, evidence-based information about treatment of substance use. Once a member, you will also become part of my Keep Calm and Treat Addiction community, where you will be invited to join VIP trainings and events.

Email tania@taniakellyhealth.com.au to request your complimentary access.

OFFER 2

Keep calm and host a workshop

TANIA KELLY
is the author of Keep Calm and Treat Addiction

A highly sought after skilled speaker, Tania has helped many professionals understand addiction, and gain confidence in recognising and supporting people struggling with drug and alcohol issues. Tania can specifically design and deliver a package for your workplace, community group or education setting.

Tania is a Credentialled Mental Health Nurse and Tobacco Treatment Specialist. She has a Post Graduate Diploma in Mental Health Nursing and is an authorised SMART Recovery Facilitator, experienced in facilitating both face to face and online groups. After 24 years in a diverse nursing career, in 2013 Tania discovered a passion for supporting people in their mental health and addiction journeys, and has established her own nurse-led clinic, Tania Kelly Health Consultant in Mackay. In addition to private practice, her counselling experience spans across a variety of treatment environments inclusive of inpatient, outreach and community-based settings.

Tania's experience in owning and co-managing a Smash Repair business equips her to understand industry and business, and the challenges substance use poses to managers in the workplace. Furthermore, her years of experience working with adolescents in high school settings, places her well-prepared to understand the demands and challenges substance use creates for educators and support staff.

Responding to alcohol and other drug issues in the workplace

- Why the workplace should respond to alcohol and other drug issues
- Types of drugs, their effects and potential consequences for the workplace
- Workplace alcohol and other drug policy
- Prevention and intervention

Recognising problematic drug and alcohol use and supporting change

- Types of drugs and their effects
- Cycle of addiction
- Addiction and the brain
- Accessible supports and treatments

Alcohol and other drugs in schools

- Whole school approach to drug and alcohol prevention
- Evidence based alcohol and drug education in the classroom
- Practical steps on responding to alcohol and other drug incidents
- How to support young people and their families affected by drug and alcohol use

✉ tania@taniakellyhealth.com.au   🌐 www.taniakellyhealth.com.au   📞 +61 428 480 295

OFFER 3
Keep calm and get individualised workplace consultancy

Tania offers individual consultancy packages to workplaces and organisations on a range of work-related drug and alcohol issues including but not limited to:

- workplace alcohol and other drug policies and procedures
- workplace alcohol and other drug intervention strategies
- employee awareness and education sessions (designed with your workplace in mind)
- occupational health and safety staff training programs specific to your organisation
- evaluation of education, training, and intervention strategies.

Tania's consultancy customers also receive unlimited email support and lifetime access to members area, where AOD resources can be accessed.

Email tania@taniakellyhealth.com.au to discuss a package to suit your needs.

Notes

Keep Calm and Treat Addiction

Notes